HOW TO READ
THE PSALMS

TREMPER LONGMAN III

InterVarsity Press
Downers Grove, Illinois
Leicester, England

InterVarsity Press, USA
P.O. Box 1400, Downers Grove, IL 60515-1426, USA
World Wide Web: www.ivpress.com
E-mail: mail@ivpress.com

Inter-Varsity Press, England
38 De Montfort Street, Leicester LE1 7GP, England
World Wide Web: www.ivpbooks.com
E-mail: ivp@uccf.org.uk

InterVarsity Press®, U.S.A., is the book-publishing division of InterVarsity Christian Fellowship/USA®, a student movement active on campus at hundreds of universities, colleges and schools of nursing in the United States of America, and a member movement of the International Fellowship of Evangelical Students. For information about local and regional activities, write Public Relations Dept., InterVarsity Christian Fellowship/USA, 6400 Schroeder Rd., P.O. Box 7895, Madison, WI 53707-7895, or visit the IVCF website at <www.ivcf.org>.

Inter-Varsity Press, England, is the book-publishing division of the Universities and Colleges Christian Fellowship (formerly the Inter-Varsity Fellowship), a student movement linking Christian Unions in universities and colleges throughout the United Kingdom and the Republic of Ireland, and a member movement of the International Fellowship of Evangelical Students. For information about local and national activities write to UCCF, 38 De Montfort Street, Leicester LE1 7GP.

Cover illustration: Roberta Polfus

Printed in the United States of America ∞

Library of Congress Cataloging-in-Publication Data

Longman, Tremper.
  How to read the Psalms.

  Bibliography: p.
  1. Bible. O.T. Psalms—Criticism, interpretation,
etc. I. Title.
BS1430.2.L66 1988   223'.206 88-8835
ISBN 0-87784-941-2

British Library Cataloguing in Publication Data

Longman, Tremper
  How to read the psalms.
  1. Bible. O.T. Psalms – Critical studies
  I. Title 223'.206

  ISBN 0-85110-787-7

P	29	28	27	26	25	24	23	22	21	20	19	18
Y	16	15	14	13	12	11	10	09	08	07	06	05

To my parents,
Tremper and Mernie Longman

Preface

The Psalter is one of the most familiar and most foreign of books in the Bible. It is familiar to us from constant exposure in both private and public devotional readings. It is foreign to us because of its poetic idiom and its implicit setting. It is my prayer that this book will help its readers understand the Psalter better.

I have had a broad readership in mind as I have written the book. I hope it can be used both inside and outside of an academic setting. I tried to make the book readable for the college student while still providing enough substance to make it appropriate for a seminary course on Psalms. I also hope that it will be studied by adult Sunday-school classes as well as interested individuals.

Many chapters end with some questions for further thought and a bibliography. An answer key for the questions is provided at the end of the book. The last few chapters omit questions because their content is too involved for brief questions and answers. The bibliographies are intended for those who want to pursue the study of a particular subject further. Some books are marked with an asterisk to indicate that they are highly technical studies.

I want to take this opportunity to thank a number of individuals who gave me help while I was writing this book. Some of my colleagues at Westminster Theological Seminary took time from their busy schedules to read the manuscript and offer me constructive criticism. I would like to thank Drs. Raymond Dillard, Sinclair Ferguson, Moises Silva and Bruce Waltke for their comments and encouragement. Professor Terry Eves of Calvin College also provided me with much helpful advice. My good friend and fellow elder at New Life Presbyterian Church (Jenkintown, Pennsylvania), Mr. Richard Wyatt, also read the manuscript and provided me with comments on substance and style. While benefiting from their comments, needless to say, I accept full responsibility for any errors (particularly since I didn't act on all of their suggestions).

Most of all, I would like to express my thanks and affection to my wife, Alice, and my three children (Tremper IV, Timothy and Andrew) for their support while I worked on this and other projects.

I dedicate this book to my parents, Tremper (Jr.) and Mernie Longman, for the loving way in which they raised me.

Introduction:
An Invitation
to the Psalms

God is present in every corner of his creation. He is with us whether we are at work or at home, shopping or studying, in the city or in the country, at sea or on land. He is everywhere and with us no matter what we do.

Nonetheless, the Scriptures make it clear that, though God's presence permeates the world, he chooses to dwell in a special way in certain places and to make his presence known at certain times. For instance, the Lord dwelt on Mount Sinai (Ex 19—20) in a special way at the time that Moses received the law. His presence was manifested and experienced in a way that was not repeated on any other mountain until he chose to dwell on Mount Zion in the time of Solomon.

These special places of God's presence are places of intimate and at times fearful encounter with the God of the universe. They are places which demand human response; they demand worshipful prayer. The Psalms are such a divine-human encounter, and they find their actual setting within the formal worship of Israel.

As we read the Psalms, we are entering into the sanctuary, the place where God meets men and women in a special way.

We will see that the conversation between God and his people is direct, intense, intimate and, above all, honest.

Thus, the Psalms are a kind of literary sanctuary in the Scripture. The place where God meets his people in a special way, where his people may address him with their praise and lament. In the same way that the sanctuaries of the Old Testament, primarily the tabernacle and the temple, were considered to be at the physical center of the people of God, so too is the book of Psalms in the middle of the Bible.

Moreover, there is a second connection between the Psalms and the sanctuary. It is here that the Psalms found their use during the Old Testament period, that is, within the context of the community and private worship of God. The Psalms were sung in the temple on Mount Zion:

Praise awaits you, O God, in Zion;
    To you our vows will be fulfilled.
We are filled with the good things of your house,
    of your holy temple. (Ps 65:1, 4)

In the Psalter we see the Old Testament people of God at worship.

This connection between the Psalms and intimate worship of God accounts at least in part for the tremendous appeal which the book has for us as Christians. While Christians have always struggled to understand and apply the Old Testament to their lives, the Psalms have found wide use in the church and in private devotions.

As a result the Psalms, more than most parts of the Old Testament, are used in the context of worship today. In recognition of this fact, publishers produce pocket-sized New Testaments which include the Psalms in the back. Moreover, many contemporary Christian hymns (not to speak of more traditional hymns) are based on passages from the Psalms. Churches with a liturgical bent incorporate a responsive reading from the Psalms into the order of worship. Most significantly, while the church suffers from a lack of preaching from the Old Testament as a whole, sermons are often based on a text from the Psalter.

How have the Psalms retained their appeal through the ages? Listen to the thoughts of two of the fathers of the Protestant church:

> In the Psalms we looked into the heart of all the saints, and we seem to gaze into fair pleasure gardens—into heaven itself, indeed—where blooms in sweet, refreshing, gladdening flowers of holy and happy thoughts about God and all his benefits. (Martin Luther)

> What various and resplendent riches are contained in this treasury, it were difficult to find words to describe. . . . I have been wont to call this book not inappropriately, *an anatomy of all parts of the soul;* for there is not an emotion of which any one can be conscious that is not here represented as in a mirror. (John Calvin)[1]

The Psalms appeal to the whole person; they demand a total response. The Psalms inform our intellect, arouse our emotions, direct our wills and stimulate our imaginations. When we read the Psalms with faith, we come away changed and not simply informed. Of course, the whole of Scripture is radically life-changing, but the Psalms address the modern Christian in a more direct way than, say, the last half of Joshua which details the geographical boundaries of the twelve tribes of Israel.

The purpose of this book is to deepen our love for the Lord by increasing our understanding of this important portion of his Word. Though the Psalms speak to us, a reason we continue to use the book often in our public and private devotion, they are often difficult to understand. We shouldn't be surprised that we struggle to understand the Old Testament in general and the Psalms in particular. After all, they are distant to us in three ways: historically, culturally and theologically.

The latest psalm was written almost 2,500 years ago. The earliest psalm was probably written about 3,500 years ago. Think about that a moment. That would be like someone in A.D. 5500 reading something written today. Times change. God speaks to his people in ways and through means related to their own times.

Along with chronological distance, we must also take into

account cultural distance. Most of the people reading this book are Westerners (since it is written in English). The Psalms, however, were originally addressed to a group of Near Eastern people, the Israelites. While cultural dissimilarity should not be overplayed, since there is much continuity between cultures, we can expect that we will run into some customs and expressions that are strange to our modern, technological society.

Last, and perhaps most significant, there is theological distance. That is, the Psalms were written before Jesus Christ was born, crucified and raised. The Psalms were written in the context of temple worship and animal sacrifice. We will see that Jesus Christ is not absent from the Psalter but, nonetheless, there is a theological distance between the Psalms and the Christian. We need to be aware of this.

These three areas of distance between the Psalms and the Christian manifest themselves in particular areas of difficulty. The most notorious difficulty is the strong language of anger which some of the psalmists use. As previously noted, the psalmists are honest, even brutally frank with God, and occasionally they blast their enemies in a way that Christians feel is out of character with the God that they know through Jesus Christ.

On a more formal level, Christians may wonder at all the repitition in the Psalms. Some psalms sound very similar (for an extreme example look at Ps 14 and 53). Moreover, the lines within an individual psalm are highly repetitive. The Psalms, we must remember, are poetry, and poetry in any language is difficult to penetrate. How are we to read this poetry, this ancient poetry?

Is Jesus Christ anticipated in the Psalter and, if so, how? Are there predictive prophecies found in a few select psalms or does the book as a whole look forward to his coming? These are just a few of the issues with which we will deal in the following chapters.

The book is divided into three parts. In the first part we are asking how the Psalms were understood and used during the period of the Old Testament. We will be studying the individual psalms as a whole. With this background, we will explore how the Psalms address us today. How should we as Christians read the individual prayers and songs which make up the Psalter? In the next section we will take a close-up look at the Psalms to see the art of the psalmists and the literary devices which they used. Finally, in the last section, three psalms will be examined closely to show how our study all fits together. The chapters in parts one and two each contain numbered suggestions for psalm study that together will summarize a systematic approach for individual study of the Psalms.

As we probe the Psalms together, our ultimate purpose is not to increase our knowledge of ancient customs and poetic forms; we are studying to know God better through his Word.

Part I
The Psalms
Then and Now

1
The Genres
of the
Psalms

Come, let us sing for joy to the LORD;
    let us shout aloud to the Rock of our salvation.
Let us come before him with thanksgiving
    and extol him with music and song. (95:1-2)

Save us and help us with your right hand,
    that those you love may be delivered. (60:5)

Give thanks to the LORD, call on his name;
    make known among the nations what he has done.
Sing to him, sing praise to him;
    tell of all his wonderful acts. (105:1-2)

He who dwells in the shelter of the Most High
    will rest in the shadow of the Almighty.
I will say of the LORD, "He is my refuge and my fortress,
    my God, in whom I trust." (91:1-2)

In these short quotations we glimpse the different *types* of poems encountered in the Psalter. In order of occurrence we have an example from a hymn, a lament, a psalm of remembrance and a psalm of confidence.

We don't have to know the Psalter very well to recognize that there are different types of psalms—roughly seven basic types. Before analyzing these types, however, it is important to realize that many differences occur between psalms of the same type. In other words, we must recognize *similarities* between psalms, not cloned repetition.

Psalms is not the only Bible book which raises the question of "type" of literature. We should ask the same question when studying any portion of Scripture. Thus, the following discussion applies to our reading of the entire Bible, though we will now focus on Psalms.

What Is a Genre?

What we have been calling a *type* is more formally known as a *genre*.[1] *Genre* refers to a group of texts similar in their mood, content, structure or phraseology.

We are all aware of various genres which we are likely to encounter in our reading today. A current favorite form of recreational reading is the biography. Individual biographies have many differences, which isn't surprising since they describe the lives of dissimilar people, but each biography intends to depict the life of a particular individual.

Newspaper editorials reflect another commonly encountered genre. The list could go on and on. The textbook, the dissertation, the novel, the short story, the lyric poem, the instruction manual, the grocery list . . .

The Bible is a library of literary genres. The *letter* to the Ephesians, the *Gospel* of Mark, the *Revelation* of John, the *prophecy* of Isaiah, the book of *Chronicles*—this is just a sampling of the different types of literature found in the Bible.

We have already noted a few different types of psalms. Besides hymns, laments, psalms of remembrance and psalms of trust, we will also discover thanksgiving, wisdom and kingship psalms.

Why Bother with Genre?

It might be surprising to realize that our interpretation of a text is to a great extent determined by our identification of its genre. "That's impossible," some might say, "I have never identified a genre in my life!" Actually we identify genres every time we read.

In her book *Genre*, Heather Dubrow begins with an excerpt from a piece entitled *Murder at Marplethorpe:*

The clock on the mantelpiece said ten thirty, but someone had suggested recently that the clock was wrong. As the figure of the dead woman lay on the bed in the front room, a no less silent figure glided rapidly from the house. The only sounds to be heard were the ticking of that clock and the loud wailing of an infant.[2]

While reading, ask yourself: Who is the dead woman and how did she die? Who is the silent figure? Why is the infant crying? What is the significance of the time?

The title is the main clue that this excerpt is from a murder mystery. Thus it is likely, especially if you are an avid reader of mysteries, that you have already identified the dead woman as the murder victim and suspect that the silent figure is the murderer. The baby is likely crying because the violent murder has awakened him or her. The clock's accuracy is significant because it marks the probable time of the murder.

Clear your mind of this story now, and read the same paragraph again, except this time under the title *The Personal History of David Marplethorpe*. Ask yourself the same questions concerning the story and you'll come up with different answers. Since biographies usually open with the birth of the hero, it is most likely that the baby is David Marplethorpe. The dead woman must be his mother who has tragically died in childbirth; the silent figure is probably the midwife leaving the scene. The time is the time of Marplethorpe's birth.

This rather lengthy example from Dubrow's book illustrates well the importance of genre identification. *It determines the reading strategy* of a particular text. If you think this brief story is a murder mystery, you will read it one way. If you think it is a biography, you will interpret it differently.

Genre identification may be conscious or unconscious, but in either case it shapes interpretation. When I pick up the newspaper in the morning, I don't say to myself: "This is a newspaper and as a newspaper I am reading someone's description and interpretation of the previous day's events. I will read it believing that the events reported are true (unless there is suitable contrary evidence), even if parts must be taken with a grain (or more) of salt." Though I don't consciously think this way, it is indeed the attitude with which I read the paper.

Most of the time we read the Bible without being conscious of our genre identification. For instance, we open to the book of Ezra and read:

> King Darius then issued an order, and they searched in the archives stored in the treasury at Babylon. A scroll was found in the citadel of Ecbatana in the province of Media, and this was written on it: Memorandum: In the first year of King Cyrus . . . (Ezra 6:1-2)

The mention of the specific king, specific time, and the specific places leads us to believe we are reading history. This is a genre identification that most Bible readers make without reflection, and therefore do unconsciously.

In the same way as we begin to study Galatians, we read in the first verses:

> Paul, an apostle—sent not from men nor by man, but by Jesus Christ and God the Father, who raised him from the dead—and all the brothers with me, To the churches in Galatia. (Gal 1:1-2)

We immediately recognize that Paul is writing a letter.

We can see from these two examples how important genre identification is in our reading of Scripture. For instance, Galatians is a letter written to a particular first-century Christian community with specific problems. In his letters Paul for the most part assumes rather than explains the problems he addresses. Once we recognize that we are reading a letter, it helps us understand why we often feel like we're overhearing a conversation when we read a Pauline letter. We must reconstruct the issue which Paul is addressing before we apply the contents of the letter to our own situation.

For instance, it is difficult to reconcile Paul's thought about the law of God in Galatians 3 with some of his comments in other epistles. The first step toward understanding this passage is to recognize that Paul is confronting a specific problem (the Galatians' tendency to depend on the law) rather than writing a systematic exposition of the relationship between the law and the Christian.

From our examples we may also see how many of the debates over the interpretation of Scripture are really debates over the identification of a text's genre. For instance, is the book of Matthew history in the sense that it imparts information to us about events which took place in time and space or is it midrash (a kind of historical fiction)?[3] Is apocalyptic literature (for instance, Daniel and Revelation) composed of symbolic images or is the beast really going to appear with seven heads and ten crowns? These are genre questions.

The Genres of the Psalms

In the same way, it is important for us to ask about the genres of the psalms. Not only will genre help us in the interpretation of individual texts, it will also provide a convenient way for us to cover most of the psalms without studying each of them individually. In other words, as we study a few examples of hymns in the Psalter, it will give us insight (not an exhaustive interpretation to be sure) into all of the hymns found there. While each hymn has its own character, it also shares many traits with others of its type.

Thus, we are now going to examine the major types of psalms. It must be admitted immediately, however, that the pie may be cut in many different ways. Scholars have suggested alternative ways to list the genres of the psalms.[4] Also, a psalm may be assigned to different levels of genre from specific to general. In other words, we need to be flexible as we speak of a psalm's genre.

Toward the pole of generality, all psalms are in the genre of poetry, but our discussion now will focus on a narrower level of genre. The seven genres which we will describe are the hymn, the lament, the thanksgiving psalm, the psalm of remembrance, the psalm of confidence, the wisdom psalm and the kingship psalm. These seven genres may be broken down further into even narrower genres.

This chapter intends to explain how the various genres of psalms may be recognized. The following chapters will deal with some of the interesting issues of interpretation and application of each of these genres.

The Hymn

Praise the LORD, O my soul;
    all my inmost being, praise his holy name.
Praise the LORD, O my soul,
    and forget not all his benefits. (103:1-2)

Hymns are easily recognized by their exuberant praise of the Lord. The psalmist pulls out all the stops in his rejoicing in God's goodness. His praise is exuberant because the psalmist is very conscious of God's presence.

Though there are many different types of hymns, almost all of them share a similar basic structure.

1. Hymns begin with a call to worship.

2. They continue by expanding on the reasons why God should be praised.

3. Hymns often include, and sometimes conclude with, further calls to praise.

The psalmist begins the hymn with a *call to worship*. Usually this call is extended to other worshipers, but occasionally (as in Ps 103) it is a call to the psalmist himself to worship the Lord. A frequent opening to a hymn is the simple command to "Praise the Lord!" which in Hebrew is the familiar *Hallelu Yah*.

Praise the LORD.
Praise, O servants of the LORD,
    praise the name of the LORD. (113:1)

A variation on the theme of the call to worship is the simple assertion by the psalmist that he will offer praise to the Lord:

It is good to praise the LORD
     and make music to your name, O Most High. (92:1)
The *reasons for praise*, however, form the most significant part
of the psalm. God is not praised for abstract qualities, but rather
for the way in which he has entered into the individual and
corporate lives of his people.

It is often easy to spot the transition from the call to worship
to the reasons for worship in a hymn because the latter is
usually introduced by the Hebrew conjunction *ki* ("for" sometimes translated "because").

It is good to praise the LORD . . .
For you make me glad by your deeds, O LORD. (92:1, 4)

Sing to the LORD a new song . . .
For all the gods of the nations are idols,
     but the LORD made the heavens. (96:1, 5)

The hymns may be further divided on the basis of the reason
for the praise. For example, God is often extolled as the Creator:
     The heavens declare the glory of God;
          the skies proclaim the work of his hands.
     Day after day they pour forth speech;
          night after night they display knowledge.
     There is no speech or language
          where their voice is not heard.
     Their voice goes out into all the earth,
          their words to the ends of the world. (19:1-4)
He is also praised as King (see below on kingship psalms):
     God has ascended amid shouts of joy,
          the LORD amid the sounding of trumpets,
     Sing praises to God, sing praises;
          sing praises to our King, sing praises. (47:5-6)
An interesting twist is seen in the "Zion Songs" which extol Mt.
Zion, not because of any greatness on its part (physically, it is
rather unimposing), but because God has caused his presence

to dwell there in a special sense in the temple.
> Great is the LORD,
>> and most worthy of praise,
> in the city of our God,
>> his holy mountain.
> It is beautiful in its loftiness,
>> the joy of the whole earth.
> Like the utmost heights of Zaphon is Mount Zion,
>> the city of the Great King. (48:1-2)

The single most important reason for praise given by the psalmist is certainly that the Lord has delivered Israel out of distress. He has redeemed her from her enemies. Accordingly, we will take a close look at a hymn of deliverance (Ps 98) in the final chapter.

The Lament

As we turn to the lament, we go from the height of our relationship with God to its depths. The lament is the polar opposite of the hymn on the emotional spectrum.

Similar to the hymn, the lament genre is primarily defined by its mood.

> My God, my God, why have you forsaken me?
>> Why are you so far from saving me,
>> so far from the words of my groaning?
> O my God, I cry out by day, but you do not answer,
>> by night, and am not silent. (22:1-2)

The lament is the psalmist's cry when in great distress he has nowhere to turn but to God. We discover three types of complaints as we read through the laments.

1. The psalmist may be troubled by his own thoughts and actions.

2. He may complain about the actions of others against him (the "enemies").

3. He may be frustrated by God himself.[5]

It is widely accepted that Psalms 42 and 43 actually compose a single psalm. This theory is based on the refrain which unites them (42:5, 11; 43:5). Together these psalms illustrate all three

types of complaints which can be seen in a lament. The psalmist is concerned about himself when he moans:

Why are you downcast, O my soul?
    Why so disturbed within me? (42:5, 11; 43:5)
He also complains about his enemies:
    . . . men say to me all day long,
    "Where is your God?" (42:3)
But most frightening to him is his sense of abandonment by
God:
I say to God my Rock,
    "Why have you forgotten me?" (42:9)
One of the difficult issues in interpreting the laments is the
identity of the "enemies." Some scholars have taken them as
the national enemies of Israel, others as "sorcerers" and still
others as accusers in a legal case.

In most cases the references are vague, and we have every
reason to believe they are so intentionally. The psalms are
purposefully vague in reference to historical events so that they
can be used in a variety of situations.

Besides mood, laments are also united by a similar structure.
The following seven elements are associated with a lament,
though not strictly in the order listed here:

1. Invocation
2. Plea to God for help
3. Complaints
4. Confession of sin or an assertion of innocence
5. Curse of enemies (imprecation)
6. Confidence in God's response
7. Hymn or blessing

Rarely will all seven elements actually occur together, but a
number of them will appear in each lament.

The psalmist often begins with an *invocation* combined with
a *plea to God for help*. There is no one the psalmist can turn to
but God himself:

Help, LORD, for the godly are no more;
    the faithful have vanished from among men. (12:1)

Hear, O LORD, my righteous plea;
   listen to my cry. (17:1)

Occasionally, the plea or petition will occur separately from the invocation (see the in-depth analysis of Ps 69 in chapter ten).

The *complaint* is a focal point of the lament psalm because it is here that we learn what has motivated the psalmist to prayer.

But I am a worm and not a man,
   scorned by men and despised by the people.
All who see me mock me;
   they hurl insults, shaking their heads. (22:6-7)

Though the mood of the lament is generally melancholic, there are one or two moments when the psalmist makes clear his basic trust in God. This is true of the section in which the psalmist expresses his confidence:

Surely God is my help;
   the Lord is the one who sustains me. (54:4)

Since a lament predominantly reflects a downcast mood, it is surprising to note that all laments include some *expression of trust in God.*

The curse on the enemies (imprecation) is perhaps the most difficult part to reconcile with our feelings about God. A particularly hard-hitting imprecation is found in Psalm 109:

May his days be few;
   may another take his place of leadership.
May his children be fatherless
   and his wife a widow. (vv. 8-9)

A fuller discussion of the role of the curse in Psalms may be found in chapter ten in connection with Psalm 69.

Laments may be further divided on the basis of whether the psalmist *confesses his sin* in the context of his suffering or, the opposite, *protests his innocence.*

You know my folly, O God;
   my guilt is not hidden from you. (69:5)
I abhor the assembly of evildoers
   and refuse to sit with the wicked. (26:5)

As Christians, we resonate with the confession but find the

psalmist's assertion of innocence almost presumptuous. We are offended by the latter because we think of Paul's strong statements on the total sinfulness of men and women (Rom 3:9-20). But we must remember that there are occasions when people are persecuted or harassed in situations or for reasons for which they are totally innocent. Assertions of innocence do have a proper place in the context of prayer.

Last, *hymns of praise* are common toward the conclusion of a lament. As the psalmist realizes what God can and will do for him, it leads him to praise God:

My feet stand on level ground;
    in the great assembly I will praise the LORD. (26:12)

The transition from complaint to praise is often so abrupt that many scholars feel that laments presuppose the presence of a priest. As the primary setting of the Psalms is in the formal worship service, the priest would hear the complaint and then respond with an assurance of pardon and God's help. This assurance would allow the psalmist to respond in joy. The priest's statements, so the argument runs, were not recorded in the psalm. This reconstruction seems reasonable, though the important point to notice is that sorrow turns to joy in most laments.

As we read a psalm, we are often able to differentiate individual laments from national laments. To do so helps us to reconstruct how the psalm was understood by the ancient Israelites. Psalm 83 is without a doubt a national lament. The enemy is a coalition of nations seeking to destroy Israel.

Most laments are individual in the sense that the psalmist speaks in the first-person singular *I*.

I lie down and sleep;
    I wake again, because the LORD sustains me.
I will not fear the tens of thousands drawn up
        against me on every side.
Arise, O LORD!
    Deliver me, O my God!
Strike all my enemies on the jaw;
    break the teeth of the wicked. (3:5-7)

On the surface, Psalm 3 appears to be a true individual lament.
However, in another sense it is actually a community lament.
The *I* is David, the king of Israel. As king, his enemies are the
community's enemies. Psalm 3 was probably primarily used in
the context of Israel's battles against foreign incursion.[6]

Thanksgiving Psalms

A review of the lament form in the Psalter naturally leads to a
consideration of songs of thanks. The lamenter sometimes explicitly promises his thanks if God will hear his voice:

I am under vows to you, O God;

   I will present my thank offerings to you. (56:12)

Further, the praise of God which is found in so many laments
anticipates that God will hear and answer the psalmist's urgent
plea for help. When he does, the psalmist lifts his voice once
again to offer thanks.

The desire to express gratitude to the Lord for answered
prayer is frequently seen in the Psalter and occasionally in the
historical books. For example, Hannah prays for a son and
promises that she will "give him to the LORD for all the days
of his life, and no razor will ever be used on his head" (1 Sam
1:11). Hannah fulfilled her obligation of thanks to God when
she gave Samuel to Eli.

The thanksgiving psalm is a response to answered lament. In
addition, there is a close connection between hymns and
thanksgivings. The relationship is so close, in fact, that Westermann has argued well that thanksgiving is really a subcategory
of praise.[7] A thanksgiving psalm is praise to God for answered
prayer.

A typical thanksgiving *begins in a similar way to a hymn of
praise.* The psalmist declares his intention to praise God:

I will extol the LORD at all times;

   his praise will always be on my lips. (34:1)

Some thanksgivings, however, begin with a blessing:

Blessed is he

   whose transgressions are forgiven,

   whose sins are covered. (32:1)

The psalmist, thanking the Lord for answered prayer, bears witness to God's great work in his life. He even calls on the rest of the congregation to join him in thanking the Lord:

Sing to the LORD, you saints of his;
    praise his holy name. (30:4)

The thanksgiving is most easily identified by a *restatement of the lament* which is now answered:

The cords of the grave coiled around me;
    the snares of death confronted me.
In my distress I called to the LORD;
    I cried to my God for help. (18:5-6)

This, then, is followed by an account of God's salvation. In the case of Psalm 18 this deliverance is presented in a dramatic picture of the appearance of God as a warrior who "reached down from on high and took hold of me" (18:16). The remainder of the thanksgiving psalm continues to praise the Lord and to call on others to praise him.

Psalms of Confidence

The psalmist frequently expresses his trust in God's goodness and power. His confidence in God is present as he sings hymns of joy (Ps 46) and as he mourns (3:3-6; 52:8). Occasionally, his feelings of trust dominate the whole psalm, and these psalms we call psalms of confidence.

At least nine psalms (Ps 11; 16; 23; 27; 62; 91; 121; 125; 131) are bound together in such a genre. Tone and content, rather than structure, bring them together.

In psalms of confidence the psalmist asserts his trust in God, though enemies or some other threat are present (11:2; 23:5). Under such conditions, he is able to be at peace because his God is with him (11:4; 23:4).

These psalms contain striking metaphors which show an intimate awareness of God's presence on the part of the psalmist. God is the psalmist's refuge (11:1; 16:1), shepherd (23:1), light (27:1), rock (62:2) and help (121:2).

The submissive trust which the psalmist puts in the Lord is nowhere more movingly expressed than in Psalm 131:

I have stilled and quieted my soul;
  like a weaned child with its mother,
  like a weaned child is my soul within me. (v. 2)

Psalms of Remembrance

Psalms do not have a specific historical setting. Nonetheless, they frequently make reference to the great redemptive acts of the past. Two events particularly are cited often: the Exodus, which could be called the paradigm salvation event of the Old Testament (Ps 77:16), and the establishment of the Davidic dynasty through covenant (Ps 89 and 132). In many psalms, only one event will be cited.

Psalms of remembrance are those in which God's past acts of redemption are the focus of attention. In such psalms, a series of God's acts will be recounted. Examples of this genre are Psalms 78, 105, 106, 135 and 136.

These psalms are united in their subject matter, the "wonderful acts" of God (105:2). Nowhere in the Bible is history reported only to impart historical information, but this is especially true in the Psalms. Rather, God's acts are recounted so that Israel might praise him:

Give thanks to the LORD, call on his name;
  make known among the nations what he has done. (105:1)
Psalm 136 is unique in the Bible due to its recurrent refrain, "His love endures forever." Each verse brings a past act of God's redemption to remembrance. This is followed by the refrain. For instance, verse 13:

to him who divided the Red Sea asunder
  His love endures forever.
Psalm 78 moves beyond praise and explicitly uses redemptive history to instruct future generations how to act:

Then they [future generations] would put their trust in God
  and would not forget his deeds
  but would keep his commands. (v. 7)

Wisdom Psalms

In thinking of biblical wisdom, we normally turn to books like

Proverbs, Job, Song of Songs and Ecclesiastes. In these books we read in concrete ways how God wants us to live our lives. They reveal God's will in the nitty-gritty and difficult areas of our lives.

Certain themes emerge from these books that students of the Bible recognize as especially (though not exclusively) related to wisdom. Some of these themes are also prominent in certain psalms which we label the wisdom psalms.

The wisdom books of the Bible emphasize a contrast in ways of living which bring about different consequences. On the one hand, there are wicked men who are cursed of God, and on the other hand, there are righteous men on whom God grants his blessing (for example, read Prov 8 and 9). Such a contrast is also clear in Psalm 1:

Blessed is the man
  who does not walk in the counsel of the wicked. . . . (v. 1)
For the LORD watches over the way of the righteous;
  but the way of the wicked will perish. (v. 6)

Proverbs in particular is devoted to spelling out the alternatives between wicked (foolish) and righteous (wise) behavior. In this we may see a close connection with law. A few psalms meditate on the beauty and wonder of the law of God:

The law of the LORD is perfect,
  reviving the soul.
The statutes of the LORD are trustworthy,
  making wise the simple. (19:7)

Psalm 119 is perhaps the best-known example, devoting 176 verses to extolling God's law.

The wise men of Israel were also fascinated with the order of God's world as manifested in his creation. We have already mentioned those psalms which reflect on God's creation under the general category of the hymn, but it is also appropriate to see their connection with wisdom psalms:

The heavens declare the glory of God;
  the skies proclaim the work of his hands. (19:1)

In addition, one strain of wisdom thought deals with the more skeptical side of life and faith. Job wrestles with the difficult issue of the suffering of an apparently righteous man, and Ecclesiastes deals with the doubt of a wise man gone bad.

The psalmist who composed Psalm 73 echoes momentarily this doubting strain when he questions God about the wicked who "have no struggles; their bodies are healthy and strong" (v. 4).

Even the Song of Songs, that provocative hymn of praise to God for intimate human love, has an analog in the Psalter. Psalm 45 revels in the marriage of the king.

> All glorious is the princess within her chamber;
>> her gown is interwoven with gold.
> In embroidered garments she is led to the king;
>> her virgin companions follow her and are brought to you.
> They are led in with joy and gladness;
>> they enter the palace of the king. (vv. 13-15)

Kingship Psalms

The kingship psalms, often included under the category of hymns, may also be profitably read as an independent genre. Two groups of kingship psalms must be distinguished. First, we have in the Psalter a number of psalms which focus on the human king of Israel. The content of these psalms varies greatly. Psalm 20 calls a blessing down upon the king, Psalm 21 expresses the king's thanks and trust in the Lord. Psalm 45 (which we have already seen in another connection) rejoices in the king's wedding. The royal aspect of the psalm may not be readily apparent, because the king may refer to himself as *I* rather than as *the king*.

The second group of kingship psalms proclaim that God is king. The two subgroups are closely related because, after all, the human king was simply God's earthly reflection. God was the true king!

> For God is the King of all the earth;
>> sing to him a psalm of praise. (47:7)

Many divine kingship psalms praise God as king in connection with military victory and may also be studied as Divine Warrior hymns, as we will shortly see in Psalm 98.

Conclusion

Hymns, laments, thanksgivings, psalms of remembrance (sometimes called redemptive-historical psalms), psalms of confidence, wisdom psalms and kingship psalms—what an incredible variety of songs Israel sang to her God! Nearly every psalm in the Psalter can be understood within these categories.

A word of caution, however. Genres are not written on tablets of stone; they are flexible. Psalms may be profitably studied under more than one of our stated genres. Psalm 45 is a kingship psalm, wisdom psalm and hymn. Psalm 78 is both a psalm of remembrance and also a wisdom psalm:

I will open my mouth in parables,
I will utter hidden things, things from of old. (v. 2)

But the point is well established. The psalms are not completely isolated from one another but have many features in common. There is no such thing as a completely unique psalm!

The identification of the basic genres of psalms leads us to the question of their use or function in ancient Israel. How did our spiritual predecessors, the Israelites, use the Psalms? This is the subject of the next chapter, and it will give us clues to the relevance of the Psalms in our lives today.

Suggestions for Psalm Study

1. Consciously make a decision about the genre of a passage of Scripture as you read it.

2. Be flexible in your understanding of a text's genre. More than one category may be applicable.

3. While reading a hymn, look for the word *for* or *because*. Here we usually can find the reasons for praise.

4. As you study a hymn, list the psalmist's reasons for praise.

5. In a lament, identify the object of the psalmist's complaint. Does he focus on himself, his enemies or God?

6. Examine the structure of a lament for the presence of the seven "building blocks" (invocation, plea, complaint, expression of confidence, confession of sin or assertion of innocence, imprecation, hymn or blessing) which often occur in laments.

7. Study a lament carefully to determine whether it is the cry

of an individual or the community.

8. Once you've identified a thanksgiving psalm, try to understand the prayer (usually a quoted lament) which has been answered.

9. In a psalm of confidence, identify the factors which threaten the psalmist's well-being.

10. Identify the images of God which the psalmist uses to communicate his confidence in God as he faces trouble.

11. A psalm of remembrance is one in which the mighty acts of God are recounted. As you read a remembrance psalm, list the mighty acts of God and read about these events in the historical books of the Bible.

12. Since there is a strong connection between the wisdom books and the Psalms, ask yourself if wisdom themes—like creation order, law, the contrast between the righteous and the wicked—are present in the psalm which you are studying.

13. Examine a psalm to see if the king is speaking the prayer or is the object of prayer.

Exercises

1. Identify the genres of Psalms 34, 55, 85, 95, 135.

2. Examine the structure of Psalm 54 closely. What kind of psalm is it? How can you tell from its structure?

3. Not all the psalms fit neatly into a clear category. Read Psalm 40 closely. What genres can you associate it with?

Further Reading

Anderson, B. W. *Out of the Depths: The Psalms Speak to Us Today.* Philadelphia: Westminster Press, 1983.

Brueggemann, W. *The Message of the Psalms.* Minneapolis: Augsburg, 1984.

*Gerstenberger, E. "Psalms." In *Old Testament Form Criticism*, pp. 179-224. San Antonio, Texas: Trinity University Press, 1974.

Miller, Jr., P. D. *Interpreting the Psalms.* Philadelphia: Fortress, 1986.

Westermann, C. *The Psalms: Structure, Content and Message.* Minneapolis: Augsburg, 1980.

——————— , *Praise and Lament in the Psalms.* Atlanta: John Knox Press, 1981.

—————————

Throughout the Further Reading lists, asterisks are used to indicate books which are highly technical studies.

2
The Origin, Development and Use of the Psalms

Now that we have learned to detect different types of songs in the Psalter, we stand amazed, not only at the many different types, but also at their apparent lack of order! If we start reading with Psalm 20 and continue in order, we encounter an individual lament, a kingship hymn, a second lament for the individual and a psalm of confidence. Why are the Psalms in this apparent disorder?

This question leads to a second, related question. How did the individual psalms come into being? Did David write all of the poems? If not, then who did?

Last, how were the Psalms used by the Old Testament people of God? The answer to this question will be the first step toward solving how we, as God's new covenant people, should use them.

These are the questions this chapter will explore—questions of the origin, development and use of the Psalms. Of course, there are many aspects of this question which we cannot answer. We get only rare glimpses of the Hebrew psalm writers in action. But the Psalter and the historical books of the Old Testament do provide some clues.

The Titles

One hint concerning the origin of psalm writing comes from the titles. The titles introducing individual psalms give information about the author, the historical occasion which prompted the writing, the melody, the psalm's function and, occasionally, other matters.

Titles are frequent in the psalter. Indeed psalms which don't have an authorship title are called "orphan" psalms (such as Ps 33). Very few psalms, however, have titles which incorporate all of the information just mentioned. Most English translations make it appear as if the titles are only loosely connected to the psalms themselves, but this is not true in the Hebrew, where the titles usually constitute the first verse!

Our interest here really focuses on two types of titles: authorship and historical occasion.[1] The title of Psalm 3 contains both:

A psalm of David. When he fled from his son Absalom.

The title implies David wrote Psalm 3 in response to a very definite event in his life recorded in 2 Samuel 15:13-37. And, indeed, the content of the psalm makes sense in light of that tragic time when his own son challenged him and chased him out of his city, Jerusalem.

In the history of psalm interpretation, however, many have challenged the accuracy of the authorship titles, particularly those connected with David. The titles ascribe the largest portion of the psalms to King David. Indeed, so many psalms are cited as Davidic that some think that all the psalms were written by him, which is clearly wrong, since psalms are also attributed to the sons of Korah, to the sons of Asaph, to Solomon and even to Moses. Further, many are without ascription.

The argument against Davidic authorship was particularly strong in the early twentieth century when many believed almost all of the psalms were written late in the history of Israel, after the exile.[2] Since David lived half a millennium before the postexilic period, his authorship would be problematical, to say the least.

In spite of this earlier critical consensus, the biblical witness

to David's role in the development of worshipful song-singing
is so strong that it is hard today to imagine why so many dis-
puted it. When David is introduced in 1 Samuel 16 and 17, he
appears as a young man with two special gifts which will later
characterize his leadership. The second story tells how God
used the boy David to defeat a superior enemy, Goliath. The
first story tells how the youth used unusual musical gifts to
soothe Saul's tormented mind. This story anticipates the one
who later calls himself "Israel's singer of songs" (2 Sam 23:1).

It is true that the Hebrew phrase translated in many English
versions as *of David* can also be translated *to David* or *for David*.
Hebrew prepositions are slippery things without a context! The
argument has been forcefully made that these psalms are Davidic, not in the sense that he wrote every one with his name
connected with it, but because the majority of psalms were written in the style which he established. For instance, a Miltonic
ode is not necessarily an ode written by Milton, but one written
in his style.

A title like that found in Psalm 18, however, leaves little doubt
as to its authorship, especially when it is remembered that
Psalm 18 has as its pair David's song of praise in 2 Samuel 22.
The authorship title is connected with a historical title which
reflects the understanding that *Of David* means "composed by
David":

Of David the servant of the LORD. He sang to the LORD the
words of this song when the LORD delivered him from the
hand of all his enemies and from the hand of Saul.

In brief, we have little reason in principle to doubt that David
wrote those psalms ascribed to him. Even most modern critical
scholars agree that, though the titles are late additions, some
psalms are Davidic and most of the psalms are early. In fact,
the early twentieth-century belief that the Psalms were very late
was bound up with a now discarded view concerning the evo-
lution of Israel's religion. It was felt that such intensely personal and spiritual prayers could not have been composed early in
Israel's religious development.

While these and other arguments establish a strong likelihood for the accuracy of authorship titles, they do not prove the canonicity of the titles, a topic which leads us to discuss the historical titles.

Historical Titles

The historical titles present us with more difficulties than the authorship titles. As a result, they should be approached more cautiously.

The historical titles at the beginning of a psalm pinpoint the event which inspired its writing. There are only fourteen historical titles (Ps 3; 7; 18; 30; 34; 51; 52; 54; 56; 57; 59; 60; 63; and 142). Despite the fact that only a few psalms enter this category, they are important in that they may provide (and certainly are often taken as providing) a glimpse at the circumstances in which the Psalms were written.

Most of the historical titles have a number of similarities. For one thing, they all concern David. Each connects a psalm with a specific event in David's life. Second, though the psalm itself often speaks in the first person, the title refers to David in the third person. This shift from third person to first person pronoun suggests that someone other than David later added these titles. Third, most of them share the same grammatical form.[3]

Scholars differ radically over the significance of the historical titles. Many feel that they have no real, or at least original, connection with the psalm.[4] It is interesting to observe how more and more titles were added to the Psalms as the years passed. Most of the psalms have titles by the time we come to the time of Christ (as evidenced by the Septuagint [second century B.C.]). And even more elaborate titles are found in the later Syriac translation of the Old Testament (Peshitta [in the early centuries A.D.]). These new titles were clearly added after the time of David.

Other scholars strongly argue that the historical titles are canonical.[5] After all, there is no textual evidence that they were not part of the text. They are canonical and, therefore, inerrant.

One cannot be dogmatic about this issue. There is no doubt

that, at the very least, the fourteen titles are early tradition and, therefore, provide valuable insights into the origin of the text. Frequently, the text's content will be illuminated by the information given in the title. The best example of this is in Psalm 51:

> When the prophet Nathan came to him after David had committed adultery with Bathsheba.

This title places the psalm within the context of David's horrible sin with Bathsheba (2 Sam 12) and after he recognizes the depths of his guilt. The title fits well with the content of Psalm 51.

However, occasionally a title seems to be in tension with the content of the psalm. If we turn back to Psalm 3, we see an example. We have already commented that the setting provided by the title and the psalm itself basically agree. In the Samuel passage (2 Sam 15:13—18:6) David is fleeing the army of his son Absalom. In Psalm 3 the psalmist beseeches God for help in the presence of attackers.

A closer examination, however, produces a more cautious analysis. David's attitude seems different in the two cases. In the psalm David displays confidence in himself and in his desire to see God crush his enemies. In the Samuel account, on the contrary, David seems quite depressed and concerned that Absalom not be harmed.

Other psalms show even more pronounced difficulties. Psalm 30 is "for the dedication of the house/temple." As we carefully study its contents, however, the most natural reading is that it is a thanksgiving offered by a person who has been healed of a serious illness (see analysis of Ps 30 in chapter eleven).

After all the evidence has been surveyed, it is best to treat the titles as noncanonical, but reliable early tradition.[6] Practically speaking, the implications for reading a psalm are twofold. We should let the psalm title initially inform the reading of a psalm. However, we shouldn't bend the interpretation of a psalm unnaturally to make it conform to the title.

While perhaps not canonical guides to interpreting psalms,

the titles do, nevertheless, provide glimpses into how the Psalms likely were originally composed. Simply stated, they were composed in response to some life situation. When the psalmist experienced God's love and salvation in his life, he sang with hymns of joy. When he experienced hardship, he composed a lament. When God answered his petition, he thanked God. When he saw God enter history once again to be with his people, he recounted the long history of God's relationship with Israel.

The amazing fact about the Psalms is that, though they were born out of particular life experiences, their content is remarkably devoid of any references to the particular events which brought them into being. Whether or not Psalm 3 was actually written at the time David fled from Absalom, there is no way we could learn that from the psalm itself. The lack of historical specificity of the Psalms is highlighted when they are compared with songs in other parts of the Old Testament. A hymn of deliverance, like Psalm 98, may be compared to another hymn of deliverance, such as Exodus 15. The historical specificity of the latter is in sharp distinction, not only to what you find in Psalm 98 but throughout the Psalms. This has tremendous implications for how we understand the Psalms in their Old Testament context and also today.

How Were the Psalms Brought Together?

When all is said and done, the Psalter is quite a varied book! We move from the highest joy to the deepest grief, from incredibly short poems (Ps 117) to extremely long ones (Ps 119). The Psalms also came into being over the whole period of time in which the Old Testament was written. Often it is hard, even impossible, to date a psalm, but according to the tradition of the titles, we have a poem as early as Moses (Ps 90). We also have psalms which reflect the return from the exile:

When the LORD brought back the captives to Zion,
    we were like men who dreamed.
Our mouths were filled with laughter,
    our tongues with songs of joy. (126:1-2)

From the time of Moses to the postexilic period covers a time span of approximately one thousand years!

But as we reflect on the overall structure of the Psalter, we don't see any immediately apparent order in subject matter or date. How are we to understand the dynamics and structure of the book of Psalms?

The key is to see the Psalter as a living, open book during the whole Old Testament period. The Psalter was in constant use individually and corporately from its very beginning. In addition, new psalms were constantly added. The additions, though, were not included systematically into the collection (as far as we can tell from the internal evidence). For instance, while some obviously late psalms, like Psalms 126 and 137, are *toward* the end, they are not at the very end.

No overall structure can be discerned, but we can recognize some important groupings and movements within the book of Psalms.

Groupings

The most obvious grouping of psalms is the division of the Psalter into five books (Ps 1—41; 42—72; 73—89; 90—106; 107—150). Five books were intentionally created to parallel the five books of Moses.

Each of the five books of the Psalms concludes with a doxology. This may be illustrated by the last verse of Psalm 41 which is a lament but ends:

Praise be to the LORD, the God of Israel,
from everlasting to everlasting.
Amen and Amen. (v. 13)

Each of the five books of the Psalter shows a preference for a particular version of the divine name. For instance, in Book I, God is addressed as Yahweh, God's personal name to Israel, 273 times. Within the same book, he is addressed as Elohim, a more generic term for God, only 15 times. The proportion between the uses of these two names is reversed in Book II. The following chart shows the use of the divine name throughout the five books of the Psalms.

	Yahweh	Elohim
Book I	272	15
Book II	74	207
Book III	13	36
Books IV and V	339	7

The second criterion for grouping in the Psalter is authorship. We find at the beginning of Book II a whole group of psalms which are associated with the sons of Korah (Ps 42—49) and a little later a number of psalms attributed to Asaph (Ps 73—83).

However, the dynamic, unclosed nature of the Psalter may be clearly noted in the Davidic psalms. Most of the Davidic psalms are found in the first two books of the Psalter and indeed Psalm 72 closes the second book with these words:

This concludes the prayers of David son of Jesse. (v. 20)

As the Psalter appears to us now, this doxology needs explanation. A number of psalms before Psalm 72 are non-Davidic (including 72), and a number of psalms after Psalm 72 are Davidic. This indicates that at one point in time there was a group of Davidic psalms which concluded with this statement, but that through time other non-Davidic psalms were added into the Davidic collection and even other psalms of David were brought in later and placed after the colophon (inscription at end of book describing its production) which appears at the end of Psalm 72.

Besides authorship, other groupings may occasionally be seen. For instance, Psalms 120—134 are grouped together because they all function as songs of ascents. (Much debate surrounds the meaning of *ascents*, but the best solution suggests that we regard these psalms as songs sung by pilgrims as they ascended the temple mount.)

In conclusion, while a single systematic structure for the whole Psalter eludes us—indeed it probably does not exist—we can observe occasional groupings of smaller groups of psalms.

Movements

In Hebrew, the book of Psalms is entitled *tehillim,* which (when translated) means "songs of praise." As we look at the psalms, though, the laments substantially outnumber the songs of praise. In what sense then is this book characterized as *tehillim?*

A close examination of the Psalter suggests an answer. A decided shift takes place as we move from the beginning of the book to its end. As we move toward the end, praise overtakes lament until at the very end of the book we have a virtual fireworks of praise. The last seven psalms are not only all hymns of praise but they, for the most part, concentrate on calling the whole world to praise God:

Praise the LORD.

Praise God in his sanctuary;

praise him in his mighty heavens.

Praise him for his acts of power;

praise him for his surpassing greatness. (150:1-2)

In a real sense, the book of Psalms moves us from mourning to joy. As it says in Psalm 126, "Those who sow in tears will reap with songs of joy" (v. 5).

The first psalm also seems relevant to the whole structure. As we open the book of Psalms, a wisdom psalm (Ps 1) immediately confronts us. Wisdom psalms are relatively uncommon. Psalm 1 deliberately places an important question before us by drawing two portraits in our minds: the portrait of the wicked man and the portrait of the wise man. The question then is posed: Which are we? As we enter the sanctuary of the Psalms to worship and petition the Lord, which side are we on?

Thus, while no overall structure can be discerned, there are signs that psalms were intentionally placed, particularly at the opening and close of the book.

One other characteristic indicates the dynamic, open character of the Psalter. As is increasingly evident, the Psalter is always relevant to the people of God. This feature is related to the lack of historical specificity already noted. However, we can still see some signs that the people of God took an old psalm and added a few verses at the end to make it even more relevant to their own situation.

For instance, at the end of Psalm 51, which we have already seen is a Davidic psalm, we read these words:

In your good pleasure make Zion prosper;
    build up the walls of Jerusalem. (v. 18)
Another well-known Davidic psalm concludes:
    for God will save Zion
    and rebuild the cities of Judah. (69:35)
Both of these are best taken as references to the postexilic situation of the people of God, 400 or more years after the time of David. "Updating" may be a new concept for some readers as applied to the Psalms. However, it is a traditional explanation for such things as the addition of the account of Moses' death (Deut 34) to a book he authored.

In conclusion, then, we see that the Psalter was an open, dynamic book during the Old Testament period. The question now arises: How was it used?

How Were the Psalms Used?

This is obviously an important question as we approach the issue of the proper use of the Psalms today. We don't want to use the Psalms in a way counter to God's intended purpose for them.

Of course, all literature has more than one purpose, and the psalms may be used in many ways. Nevertheless, it is important for us to concentrate on the main ways in which they were used and along the way to point out some incorrect answers to this question.

Beyond a shadow of a doubt, the Psalms were used in the public and private worship of devout Israelites. We might even go a step further and, while affirming that the Psalms were used in private worship, say that most of the evidence for their primary use points to public worship. Indeed, the Psalms have appropriately been called "The Hymnbook of the Old Testament."

Many indications lead us in this direction. First Chronicles 16:7 mentions that David gave one of his psalms to Asaph and his associates. Asaph was the chief of the Levites who were "to minister before the ark of the LORD, to make petition, to give thanks, and to praise the LORD" (1 Chron 16:4). Some of the psalm titles link the psalms with formal worship, "For the Sabbath day" (Ps 92).

In this connection, we should also mention those fifteen songs of ascents (Ps 120—134), which are best taken as procession hymns, hymns sung by worshipers as they approached Jerusalem and the temple.

Perhaps most helpful are the references within psalms to specific acts of worship which either go along with the psalm or will follow afterward:

But I, by your great mercy,
    will come into your house;
in reverence will I bow down
    toward your holy temple. (5:7)

I will come to your temple with burnt offerings
    and fulfill my vows to you—
vows my lips promised and my mouth spoke when I
        was in trouble. (66:13-14)

I have seen you in the sanctuary
    and beheld your power and your glory.
Because your love is better than life,
    my lips will glorify you. (63:2-3)

The Psalms were sung as part of Israel's formal worship. This does not mean that the faithful in the Old Testament could not make use of the Psalms in their private worship. After all, many

of us sing praise to God during our private or family devotions
using songs which we learned first within the church community.

We get an example of an individual's use of the Psalms in 1
Samuel. Hannah, Samuel's mother, pours her heart out to the
Lord. While the setting of her prayer is the area around the
tabernacle (the arena of public worship), she is privately lifting
up her voice to God in prayer (1 Sam 1:12-14). When her lament
is answered, she then offers up a prayer of praise to God (2:1-
11).

What is of particular interest in the second prayer is its connection with Psalm 113. Perhaps here we see her basing her
prayer on a well-known psalm and applying it to her own situation. This may have been common practice. That is, an individual would pattern a prayer on a well-known psalm.

The Psalm and Special Festivals

Thus, the primary setting and use of the Psalms is within the
context of worship. Some scholars want to take this insight a
step further and argue that the Psalms are associated specifically with an annual festival.

The first to propose this was the famous psalm interpreter
Sigmund Mowinckel.[7] Mowinckel correctly showed that the
Psalms found their home in the context of formal worship, but
then went on to say that the Psalms were part of a New Year's
festival in Israel during which God was re-enthroned and again
proclaimed as king.

Direct evidence for such a festival is lacking in the Bible, and
Mowinckel had to appeal to Babylonian practices to make his
case. Accordingly, his ideas concerning an enthronement ceremony are accepted by very few today.

Nonetheless, numerous other commentators on the Psalms
have proposed alternative festivals in which the Psalms may
have been used. Most notably, Artur Weiser speaks of a Covenant Festival[8] and H.J. Kraus reconstructs a Zion Festival from
the Psalms.[9]

While there may have been an annual or more occasional

recommitment to the covenant on the part of Israel, one must be cautious to find the primary setting of the Psalms in a hypothetical festival. The Psalms were part of the worship of Israel, both corporate and individual. As such, they probably were used during the festivals, but the Psalms functioned more generally than this. They were used as Israel rejoiced and mourned. They were always relevant to Israel because they are not historically specific and are immediately applicable to new situations of blessing and curse.

Conclusion

Any analogy of the Psalms with the writing and use of modern hymns is helpful, though perhaps not exact. Each psalm was probably born of specific experience. For example, David was hunted by Saul and wrote a prayer of lament to God in response (Ps 54). The prayer, however, was not historically specific. He wrote:

Save me, O God, by your name . . .

Not:

Save me from Saul, O God, by your name . . .

Thus, the psalm was continually relevant, not just to David, but to anyone who experienced trouble. The psalm entered into the formal worship where the priests and Levites could guide and teach the worship of God. Individuals could then use them privately as well.

Suggestions for Psalm Study

14. Let the psalm title initially inform the reading of a psalm.

15. Don't bend the interpretation of a psalm unnaturally to make it conform to the title.

16. Examine the last verses of a psalm to see if there is any evidence that the psalm was "updated."

Exercises

1. Read the title of Psalm 52 and then the psalm itself. How do the two relate? Remind yourself of the story by reading 1 Samuel 21:1-9; 22:6-23.

Further Reading

Eaton, J. H. *The Psalms Come Alive.* Downers Grove, Ill.: InterVarsity Press, 1986.

Kidner, D. *Psalms.* Tyndale Old Testament Commentaries. Downers Grove, Ill.: InterVarsity, Press, 1973.

3
The Psalms:
The Heart of
the Old Testament

Some books of the Bible are hard to find! When a minister calmly asks the congregation to turn to Nahum, panic spreads throughout the pews. No such problem occurs with the book of Psalms. Besides being one of the longest books of the Bible, it is located at the heart or center of the Bible. By opening your Bible to the middle, you usually open to the Psalms.

But the Psalms are at the heart of the Old Testament in a far more important way as well. The Psalms are the heart of the message of the Old Testament. In this chapter, we will examine the message of the book of Psalms.

First, however, a word of caution. This chapter can only be understood within the context of the next chapter. While this chapter explores the message of the Psalms within its Old Testament context, the next chapter shows how the coming of Jesus Christ transforms our understanding of the Psalms.

Further, in this chapter and the next, the emphasis is on the message or theology of the Psalms. Once again, we must keep in mind that this is only part of their appeal. Chapter five will continue our study of their message by demonstrating how the book appeals to more than our minds. The Psalter stimulates our imagination, arouses our emotions and appeals to our wills. Reading the Psalms touches the very core of our being.

The Old Testament in the Psalms
Of course, it is stating the obvious to say that the book of Psalms is in the Old Testament. It is more significant to discover that the Old Testament is in the Psalms! It has long been recognized that the Psalms are a "microcosm" of the message of the Old Testament. The fourth-century theologian Athanasius called the Psalms "an epitome of the whole Scriptures." Basil, the Bishop of Caesarea in the fourth century, noted that the Psalms were "a compendium of all theology." Martin Luther, the well-known reformer of the sixteenth century, aptly called the Psalms "a little Bible, and the summary of the Old Testament."[1]

Think about this. There are psalms which extol God's creation of the world. In addition, we learn that he providentially cares for the world. We are further instructed that the "wages of sin is death" (Rom 6:23) and that God redeems his wayward people. We hear about God's law and his wisdom. Moreover, we see that God blesses his people and curses his enemies. The Psalms teach that the righteous will live and the wicked will die. We may surely agree with J. Anderson, the nineteenth-century translator of Calvin's *Commentary on the Psalms,* when he states that the Psalms "include illustrations of every religious truth which it is necessary for us to know."[2]

However, while the Psalms contain "illustrations of every religious truth," the book is far from a systematic exposition of theology. As C. S. Lewis commented, "the Psalms are poems, and poems intended to be sung: not doctrinal treatises, nor even sermons."[3] We may agree with Lewis, while also admitting that, though not "doctrinal treatises," the Psalms do teach doctrine.

Many people associate theology with dry-bones descriptions of biblical truth. True, theologians sometimes teach and write in a boring way, but theology shouldn't be lifeless. Theology should be the expression of a person's heart and should always be applied to life situations.

Abstract theology is not found in the Bible. The whole Bible dresses truth about God in the context of our relationship with him. The historical books report what God has done for Israel (Kings, Chronicles, etc.) or the church (Acts). The prophets proclaim God as judge of the rebellious and Savior of the faithful. Paul's letters are theologically rich and at times difficult to understand, but they are always practical.

The Psalter is no exception to this rule. As a matter of fact, the Psalter represents theology in its most vibrant form.

We are not surprised, then, that the Psalter does not present a systematic picture of God and his relationship to the world. The Psalms give us theology written in intimate relationship with God and in close touch with life.

God's Covenant Relationship with Israel

To describe the theology of the Book of Psalms is, therefore, to write an Old Testament theology. We couldn't possibly do that in this short chapter. However, we can make a beginning in our understanding of the theology of the Psalms by focusing briefly on the central theological concept behind the Psalms, not to speak of the rest of the Old Testament—God's covenant with his people.[4]

Before discussing the Psalms in particular, we need to understand the biblical concept of covenant. Many people are put off by this word because it is not familiar to us from our everyday language.

As a matter of fact, *covenant* is an obsolete word. In older English, covenant was synonymous with *agreement* or *pact*. It referred to the establishment of a formal relationship between two people. In fact, the Bible uses *covenant* in this nonreligious sense. For instance, when Isaac and Abimelech made a political agreement they called it a *covenant*—a *sworn agreement* as the New International Version puts it *(bᵉrît,* Gen 26:28).

More significant for the Bible, though, the relationship between God and his people is often called a "covenant" relationship. As you might imagine, however, a covenant relationship between God and man is considerably different from one between two people. God is the Creator of men and women, after all; he doesn't enter into an "agreement" with his creatures. Rather God initiates, establishes, sets the conditions and preserves his relationship with his people.[5] He is sovereign in the relationship.

Research has revealed that a biblical covenant is closely related to political treaties from the ancient Near East.[6] Archaeologists have recovered a number of treaty documents written in Akkadian (the language of the Assyrians and Babylonians) which have been profitably compared to biblical covenants.

In these treaties, the Great King, the king of the more powerful country, initiates a political relationship with a vassal king from the less powerful country. The treaty establishes a relationship between these two countries, a relationship, though, between two unequal parties.

These treaties had a relatively set form in the ancient Near East. After the two *parties of the treaty are identified,* the treaty would continue with a history of the relationship between the two countries. In this section the emphasis usually fell on how well the Great King's country had acted toward the less powerful nation. In this way, the treaty placed a burden of gratitude on the vassal country.

The historical overview was followed by *laws* governing the future relationship between the two countries. For instance, the vassal king was commanded to come to the aid of the Great King if the latter were attacked. The Great King, in response, promised to defend his weaker treaty partner in the event that he was attacked.

Blessings and curses flowed from the law of the treaty/covenant. If one or the other of the kings broke the laws, then he would be cursed. On the other hand, if the kings were obedient, then blessings would come upon them.

At the conclusion of the treaty document, gods, people, and even heaven and earth were called on to *witness* the making of the treaty. Finally, the matter of the *deposit of the two copies* of the treaty would be dealt with.

Thus, a typical ancient Near Eastern treaty had six parts:
1. Identification of the parties making the treaty
2. Historical prolog
3. Law
4. Blessings and curses
5. Witnesses
6. Deposit of treaty text

The biblical concept of covenant is related to the Near Eastern political treaty. God often used literary forms and concepts from the ancient world to communicate with his people. Being separate in time and culture from the Old Testament world, we sometimes miss the background. Archaeological and literary study of the ancient Near East helps us to recapture the sense of the culture in which God spoke his Old Testament revelation. Thus, the discovery of ancient Near Eastern treaties has helped us to understand further the ideas behind biblical covenants.

God is the Great King who enters into a relationship with his vassal people, Israel. A number of Old Testament texts describe how God enters into a covenant relationship with his people. These texts bear a remarkable resemblance to Near Eastern treaties. For instance, Exodus 20, the entire book of Deuteronomy, Joshua 24 and 1 Samuel 12 bear a formal similarity to Near Eastern treaties.

An examination of the structure of Joshua 24 illustrates the close connection with treaties.

At the end of Joshua's life, a crisis comes upon the Israelites. They are about to lose their leader. The time is, therefore, appropriate to reaffirm their allegiance to God. They do this by means of a ceremony in which they renew the covenant. In other words, they reaffirm their relationship which they made as a nation at Mount Sinai (Ex 20).

After the two parties are assembled together and *identified* (Josh 24:1), Joshua recounts the *history of the relationship* between God and his people from the time of Abraham down to the present moment (vv. 2-13).

On the basis of God's gracious acts toward Israel, Joshua sets

down the *law* (vv. 14-15). He also lays out the *curses* which will
result from disobedience (vv. 19-20). Finally, the *witnesses* to the
covenant ceremony are cited (v. 22) and so is the matter of the
deposit of the covenant document (vv. 25-26). All of the parts of
a treaty document are present in Joshua 24. Covenant is a treaty
in the Old Testament.

The idea of covenant extends beyond literary form. The core
of the covenant idea is a relationship. God enters into a personal relationship with his people as he enters into a covenant
relationship with them. As a matter of fact, a key phrase associated with the idea of covenant in the Bible is "I will be their
God, and they will be my people."

Two important points need to be made here before we go
any further. First, we must reemphasize the truth that entering
into a relationship with God is substantially different from entering into a relationship with another person. We have already
mentioned that one reason for the difference is that God is the
Creator and we are his creatures. We don't enter into a nego-
tiated agreement with God.

Another critical reason for the difference is that God is holy
and we are sinners. Sinful people can't enter into a relationship
with a holy God. As we learn from Genesis 3, we deserve death
because of our sin. Our only hope comes from God who provides a substitute to die in our place. The ultimate substitute, of
course, is Jesus Christ, but in the Old Testament we have a
foreshadowing of Christ's death in the shedding of animal
blood. It is, therefore, pivotal to realize that at those times when
God establishes a covenant relationship with his people it is
done on the basis of a substitute death so that we can enter into
an intimate relationship with our holy God.

O. Palmer Robertson has defined covenant in his helpful
book *Christ of the Covenants* in a way which summarizes many
of the points we have made. According to Robertson a covenant
is "a bond in blood sovereignly administered."[7]

Second, some scholars give the impression that covenant permeates and explains every part of the Bible. While the covenant
idea is the most frequent metaphor found in the Bible for the

relationship between God and his people, it isn't the only one. Other metaphors of relationship are found throughout the Bible as well as in the Psalms. They are instructive to reflect on: God is our shepherd, our father, our spouse, our captain, our mother and so on.

Each metaphor highlights a different aspect of God's relationship with his people. The covenant idea emphasizes that God is our King and we are his servant people.

The Psalms as a Covenant Book

The question may already be crossing your mind: "Why is he spending so much time on covenants? I don't remember the word *covenant* occurring very often in the Psalms."

It is true that there are relatively few psalms (only twelve) which explicitly reflect on God's covenant with his people. A smaller number of psalms have covenant as a major theme (for instance, Ps 89 and 132). Nonetheless, we can't ignore the fact that the psalmists speak out of the context of covenant. These are people who speak to God and about God on the basis of being in a covenant relationship with him. Thus, covenant is a concept which ties together many strands of the theology of the Psalms. While we cannot hope to exhaust the subject, our point may be illustrated by examining selected topics. It is hoped this study will lead to further thinking about the relationship between the Psalter and covenant.

The Presence of God

Covenant bespeaks an intimate relationship with God. "I am your God; you are my people." When we enter the sanctuary of the Psalms, we know that we are in the presence of God.

We sense God's intimate presence in the shouts of rejoicing and the cries of lament in the Psalter. The psalmist knows that God hears him. He often directly addresses God. The psalmist speaks as one aware that God is with him. God is *"my* God" or *"our* God."

We also sense God's intimate, though often fearsome, presence in the numerous depictions of his coming to aid the psalmist. Note these examples:

> The earth trembled and quaked,
>   and the foundations of the mountains shook;
>   they trembled because he was angry.
> Smoke rose from his nostrils;
>   consuming fire came from his mouth,
>   burning coals blazed out of it.
> He parted the heavens and came down;
>   dark clouds were under his feet. (18:7-9)

> The voice of the LORD shakes the desert;
>   the LORD shakes the Desert of Kadesh.
> The voice of the LORD twists the oaks
>   and strips the forests bare.
> And in his temple all cry, "Glory!" (29:8-9)

God's Presence in History

God's presence with his people was no mere mystical sense of being near God. God makes his presence known to his people in space and time. He acts in history in mighty ways.

The Psalms meditate on God's past acts. They particularly call God's gracious acts of deliverance to remembrance.

> Give thanks to the LORD, for he is good.
> *His love endures forever.*
> to him who struck down the firstborn of Egypt
> *His love endures forever.*
> and brought Israel out from among them
> *His love endures forever.* (136:1, 10, 11)

Psalm 136 reflects back on the mighty act of deliverance at the time of the exodus. It attributes that act to God's love. The New International Version translates the common Hebrew word *ḥesed* as "love"; but *ḥesed* carries a more specific meaning than love. It is better translated *covenant lovingkindness*. *Ḥesed* refers to the love which results from God's intimate covenant relationship with his people.

The psalmist is not a historian. He is not interested in the past for its own sake. He reflects on God's wonderful deeds as a basis for his present confidence in the midst of trouble. For instance, in Psalm 83 the psalmist calls on God to help Israel *in the same way* that he earlier delivered Israel during the time of the Judges.

Do to them as you did to Midian,
as you did to Sisera and Jabin at the river Kishon,
who perished at Endor
and became like refuse on the ground. (vv. 9-10)

God's love is displayed in history. The recounting of acts of deliverance in the psalms functions similarly to the historical prologue of a treaty.

God Is King

At the beginning of the chapter we saw the close connection between covenant and treaty. In the ancient Near Eastern treaties a Great King made a pact with a lesser king.

Accordingly, it is not coincidental that in our covenant song book, the Psalms, that God is often extolled as a powerful king. We observed in chapter one that there is a genre of divine kingship psalms.

God is extolled in the Psalms as the king of the universe. His kingship has been and will be for all time:

The LORD reigns.
He is robed in majesty;
the LORD is robed in majesty
and is armed with strength.
The world is firmly established;
it cannot be moved.
Your throne was established long ago;
you are from all eternity. (93:1-2)

While this is true, some psalms reaffirm God's kingship in such a way that it is as though he were being crowned anew:

Clap your hands, all you nations;
shout to God with cries of joy.
How awesome is the LORD Most High,
the great King over all the earth!

He subdued nations under us,
  peoples under our feet.
He chose our inheritance for us,
  the pride of Jacob, whom he loved.
God has ascended amid shouts of joy,
  the LORD amid the sounding of trumpets. (47:1-5)
The reaffirmation of God's kingship in the psalms is often the
result of God's great deliverance of Israel (as here in Ps 47).

God's Law

Earlier, we observed the close connection between covenant
and law. God establishes a relationship with his people. In the
context of that previously established relationship, he gives
guidance to his people as to how they should live. Law plays
a significant role in our covenant Psalter. In the Psalter, as in
the covenant, God revealed his will to his people.

The psalmist, for instance, extols the wonders of the law:
The law of the LORD is perfect,
  reviving the soul.
The statutes of the LORD are trustworthy,
  making wise the simple.
The precepts of the LORD are right,
  giving joy to the heart. (19:7-8)
In this way, the psalmist appeals to God's people to remain
obedient to the covenant of God.

Two psalms explicitly relate law to the question of relationship with God:

LORD, who may dwell in your sanctuary?
  who may live on your holy hill? (15:1)

Who may ascend the hill of the LORD?
  Who may stand in his holy place? (24:3)
The answer comes in terms of law:
He whose walk is blameless
  and who does what is righteous,
  who speaks the truth from his heart. (15:2)

He who has clean hands and a pure heart,
    who does not lift up his soul to an idol
    or swear by what is false. (24:4)

Blessings and Curses

The basic principle of covenant life is that God blesses those who are obedient to his will and chastises those who aren't (compare Deuteronomy 27 and 28). One of the reasons for the presence of the book of Job in the Old Testament is to warn us against making this a dogmatic principle of retribution. Nonetheless, the people of God are encouraged to remain obedient by the promise of a continued blessed relationship.

Blessed is the man who does not walk in the
                counsel of the wicked
    or stand in the way of sinners
    or sit in the seat of mockers.
But his delight is in the law of the LORD,
    and on his law he meditates day and night.
He is like a tree planted by streams of water,
    which yields its fruit in season
    and whose leaf does not wither.
Whatever he does prospers. (1:1-3)

The next stanza of Psalm 1 describes the antithesis. As the righteous man, the man who observes the law of God, is blessed, so the wicked man is cursed.

Forgiveness

The Psalms, though, don't shirk from calling men and women sinners. Curse, not blessing, would be man's lot, if God did not intervene.

There is a group of psalms which are well known because they focus on God's forgiveness. These psalms have been called penitential psalms. Martin Luther called them the Pauline psalms. As the psalmist turns to the Lord with a repentant heart, he knows that God will forgive him.

Perhaps the most familiar of the penitential psalms is Psalm 51:

Have mercy on me, O God,
　　according to your unfailing love;
　　according to your great compassion
　　blot out my transgressions.
Wash away all my iniquity
　　and cleanse me from my sin. (51:1-2)

Conclusion

The Psalms are rich for theological meditation. We learn much about God and his ways with us as we read these inspired songs. The purpose of the Psalms, however, is not to argue, persuade or convince. Their purpose is to confess a profound faith in and love toward God. The psalmists cry out to God from the context of their intimate covenant relationship with God and they call on others who know God's love to do the same.

Suggestions for Psalm Study

17. Study the theological teaching of the psalm. What is the psalm communicating about God and his covenant relationship to his people?

Further Reading

Dumbrell, W. J. *Covenant and Creation: An Old Testament Covenantal Theology.* Exeter: Paternoster Press, 1984.

Goldsworthy, G. *Gospel and Kingdom.* Exeter: Paternoster Press, 1981.

Kaiser, W. *Toward an Old Testament Theology.* Grand Rapids: Zondervan, 1978.

Kline, M. G. *Treaty of the Great King.* Grand Rapids: Eerdmans, 1963.

*Kraus, H.-J. *Theology of the Psalms.* Minneapolis: Augsburg, 1986.

McComiskey, T. E. *The Covenants of Promise: A Theology of Old Testament Covenants.* Grand Rapids: Baker: 1985.

Robertson, O. P. *The Christ of the Covenants.* Grand Rapids: Baker, 1980.

Vos, G. *Biblical Theology.* Grand Rapids: Eerdmans, 1948.

4
A Christian Reading of the Psalms

The coming of Jesus was decisive. For Christians, Jesus splits history into two parts: B.C. and A.D. Besides being the turning point of history, Jesus is the turning point of the Bible. His coming is the decisive event of both history and Scripture.

The Old Testament is God's revelation before Jesus and the New Testament is God's revelation after Jesus. But while the Old Testament was written before Jesus, he is not absent from the Old Testament.

Jesus himself taught otherwise. After his crucifixion, two people were walking to a town near Jerusalem called Emmaus (Lk 24:13-35). Suddenly they were joined by a third person whom they didn't recognize. They were startled that this man seemed to have no knowledge of the momentous events of the previous days when Jesus was nailed to the cross.

In addition, these two followers of Christ told the stranger that some women had gone to the tomb and had found it empty! Others followed and confirmed their report. The two travelers to Emmaus were confused. What was happening?

At this point the stranger interrupted:

"How foolish you are, and how slow of heart to believe all

that the prophets have spoken! Did not the Christ have to
suffer these things and then enter his glory?" And beginning
with Moses and all the Prophets, he explained to them what
was said in all the Scriptures concerning himself. (Lk 24:25-
27)

Jesus here leaves no room for doubt. The whole Old Testament
anticipates his coming. More specifically, the entire Old Testament anticipates his suffering and his glorification.

The passage may need explanation for some. The Old Testament was for obvious reasons not called the Old Testament
in the first century. The usual way to refer to what we now call
the Old Testament was to name its main parts.[1]

In this passage, two parts are named. First of all, Jesus says
that Moses anticipated his coming suffering and glorification.
Moses here means the first five books of the Bible, the Law, the
Torah, or the Pentateuch.

The Prophets in this passage refers to the Former Prophets and
the Latter Prophets. The Former Prophets are those books we
usually identify as "historical." For example, Joshua, Judges, 1
and 2 Samuel, 1 and 2 Kings are all Former Prophets. The
Latter Prophets are those books which we normally associate
with prophets: Isaiah, Jeremiah, Ezekiel, and so on.

But where do the Psalms fit in? They are assumed in this
passage but not explicitly mentioned.[2] However they are certainly implied. If you doubt that Jesus meant to include the
Psalms in "all Scripture," turn to Luke 24:44, where the picture
becomes absolutely clear.

After the two followers on the road to Emmaus realized that
they were speaking to the risen Jesus, they immediately returned to Jerusalem and went to the remaining eleven disciples.

While they were excitedly telling the disciples of their encounter with Jesus, he appeared to them. He reminded them
of the earlier lessons they had learned:

This is what I told you while I was still with you: Everything
must be fulfilled that is written about me in the Law of Moses,
the Prophets and the Psalms. (Lk 24:44)

Here it is likely that "Psalms" included more than the book of

Psalms which we have been studying. The Old Testament canon is usually divided into three parts: the Law, the Prophets and the Writings. The Psalms stood at the front of the Writings, but also would include books like Proverbs, Song of Songs, Job and others (including, surprisingly, Daniel and Chronicles). In this passage Jesus calls the third section of the canon *Psalms* after the first book in that collection.

In any case, Jesus' language makes it absolutely certain that he believed that the Psalms anticipated his future ministry of suffering and glory.

The relationship between the Old Testament and the New Testament is a very difficult and detailed question, but for the Christian one thing is certain: Jesus is the focus of the Bible as a whole. This is not to say that the Old Testament writers had a clear and precise understanding of Jesus and his future ministry. But a future Savior was expected in the Old Testament. Immediately after the Fall, God delivered a curse upon the serpent: "I will put enmity between you and the woman, and between your offspring and hers; he will crush your head, and you will strike his heel" (Gen 3:15). As the Old Testament period continued, the expectation of a suffering, yet glorified Messiah grew stronger and stronger.

In the words of St. Augustine, "the New Testament is in the Old concealed; the Old is in the New revealed." A Savior is anticipated in the Old Testament; he is named Jesus by the New Testament.

How are we as Christians to read the Psalms? How does the coming of Christ affect our understanding of the hymns and laments?

The New Testament's Use of the Psalms

The New Testament frequently cites the Old. The Psalms are quoted more often than any other book in the New Testament.[3] We can illustrate what this means: Paul provides us with one-third of the total quotations of the Old Testament in the New Testament. One-fifth of his citations come from the Psalms.[4]

The systematic study of these quotations would require another book! However, if we did analyze them thoroughly, we would see that Paul cites the Psalms in connection with a variety of doctrines (see Rom 3:10-18; 4:6-8; 11:9-10) and not only in reference to Jesus. Our purpose is served by noting that Paul, writing from a post-Coming of Christ perspective, understood that the Psalms anticipated the Messiah who would suffer and be glorified.

In Acts 13 we find Paul in Pisidian Antioch. The leaders of the synagogue ask Paul and his friends if they would like to address the congregation. Paul accepts the invitation and preaches the gospel to them. He shows them how God had worked in the past to bring the Messiah to Israel and how the promise of the Messiah had been fulfilled in Jesus.

At the conclusion of his sermon, Paul cites four passages from the Old Testament to make his point. Two of them are from the Psalms. He applies these passages (which in their Old Testament setting referred to David and other worshipers) to Jesus:

You are my Son;

today I have become your Father. (Ps 2:7 in Acts 13:33)

You will not let your Holy One see decay. (Ps 16:10 in Acts 13:35)

Specifically, Paul quotes these passages to affirm Jesus' Sonship and his resurrection.

Paul elsewhere clearly saw that Jesus' sufferings were mirrored in the laments of the Psalms. Follow his argument in Romans 15:

We who are strong ought to bear with the failings of the weak and not to please ourselves. Each of us should please his neighbor for his good, to build him up. For even Christ did not please himself but, as it is written: "The insults of those who insult you have fallen on me." For everything that was written in the past was written to teach us, so that through endurance and the encouragement of the Scriptures we might have hope. (Rom 15:1-4, quoting Ps 69:9).

Paul read the Psalms from a Christian perspective and saw Jesus. In this, he was following the lead already set by Jesus.

Jesus himself was conscious that the Psalms anticipate his work. Jesus' horror at the sight of money changers in the temple led him forcibly to evict these trespassers. The disciples later made the connection (in Jn 2:17) with Psalm 69:9: "Zeal for your house consumes me."

Jesus saw himself in the position of the psalmist whose closest friends became his enemies: "I am not referring to all of you; I know those I have chosen. But this is to fulfill the scripture: 'He who shares my bread has lifted up his heel against me' " (Jn 13:18, quoting Ps 41:9).

At the depths of his suffering, as he hung on the cross abandoned by everyone and feeling forsaken by God himself, Jesus took upon his lips the words of the psalmist:

My God, my God, why have you forsaken me? (Mt 27:46, quoting Ps 22:1)

The New Testament thus bears witness to the effect which the coming of Jesus had on the reading of the Psalms. Questions still remain, however. Do the Psalms as a whole anticipate Jesus? Or are there special prophetic psalms which predict his suffering and glory?

The Question of Messianic Psalms

The term *messianic psalm* may be used in one of two ways. In a general sense, a messianic psalm is simply a psalm which anticipates the Messiah. We will soon see that all the psalms are messianic in this sense.

Some people, though, believe that a few psalms are messianic in the narrow sense. That is, some psalms are prophetic and have no direct message of significance for the Old Testament period. They only predict the coming Messiah.

Psalm 16 is often read as a messianic psalm in the narrow sense. The key is taken from Paul's speech in Antioch mentioned above (also cited in Peter's speech in Acts 2:25-28). Paul argues that the ultimate fulfillment of Psalm 16:10 can't be associated with David since David was dead and buried. The ultimate fulfillment came with Jesus who died but was raised "incorruptible" (to borrow language from 1 Cor 15).

However, to say that the ultimate fulfillment of Psalm 16:10 is found in Jesus' resurrection is different from arguing that the passage has no Old Testament application. A careful reading of Psalm 16 reveals that it is a song of trust in the midst of the crisis of illness. In short, the psalmist is not saying he will never die, but rather that at the time of his illness God had preserved him from death. He is sick, but he trusts God that he won't die from his illness.[5]

Jesus is anticipated in this psalm because it finds its ultimate fulfillment in him. He dies, but he is also raised. David knew that this psalm had messianic implications according to Acts 2:31. As we read the psalm from a post-Coming of Christ perspective, we see Jesus and we also see that the psalm applies to us as well since we understand what happens after we die better than the Old Testament people of God ever could.

While no psalm is exclusively messianic in the narrow sense, all the psalms look forward to Jesus Christ. How is this so?

Singing the Psalms to Our Savior

As New Testament believers, we may sing psalms to our Savior.[6] We may offer him our praise, our laments, our trust, our doubts and our meditations as we read, pray and sing the Psalms.

There are two grounds for such an approach to the Psalms. On the one hand, Jesus is the Son of God. The Psalms are offered to God and, as the second person of the Trinity, Jesus is the appropriate object of our praise and laments.

The author of Hebrews sets the pattern. In the first chapter where he cites a number of Old Testament passages to show Christ's superiority to the angels, he cites Psalm 102:25-27 in reference to Jesus (see Heb 1:8):

In the beginning, O Lord, you laid the foundations
        of the earth.
    and the heavens are the work of your hands,
They will perish, but you remain;
        they will all wear out like a garment.
You will roll them up like a robe;
        like a garment they will be changed.

But you remain the same,
    and your years will never end. (Heb 1:10-12)
In its Old Testament context, this psalm was sung to Yahweh.
From a New Testament perspective, it is correctly sung to Jesus
on the grounds that Jesus, while fully human, is fully God and
worthy of divine praise.

The second reason for singing the Psalms in praise to Jesus
is his relationship to the original singer. As we have observed,
the speaker in many of the psalms is the Davidic king. Further,
the Davidic king is often the focus of a psalm.

We must pause a moment to remind ourselves of the theology of kingship in Israel. What was the purpose of kingship in
the Old Testament? When Israel first became a nation at Mt.
Sinai, there was no human king. God was king in Israel. This
situation continued during the period of the Judges. As Samuel's judgeship was drawing to a close, however, the people
feared for the future. They were being pressed from all sides
by foreign enemies. They saw hope for the future only if they
had a king, so that they would be "like all the other nations"
(1 Sam 8:20).

The request for a king was sinful. They didn't trust God to
deliver them even though he already had delivered them from
military distress time and time again. By requesting a king, they
rejected God as their king (1 Sam 8:7).

Surprisingly, however, God tells Samuel to grant their request
and appoint a king. Though the request was sinful (because it
involved a rejection of God), the institution of kingship was not
sinful and as a matter of fact had been anticipated for centuries
(as in Deut 17:14-20).

The burning concern of 1 Samuel 8—12, then, is to establish
a human monarchy which did not infringe upon the theocracy
(God's rule as king). The conclusion comes in 1 Samuel 11:14—
12:25, which is a covenant renewal ceremony reaffirming the
nation's trust in the Lord while establishing the monarchy.[7]

The Israelite king is the human reflection of the kingship of
God. He rules because God established him as ruler. This is
particularly the case with David, with whom God made a special

covenant (2 Sam 7) establishing his kingship and his dynasty.

It is, accordingly, significant that so much of the Psalter is connected with the institution of kingship in Israel and more specifically with David and his dynasty.

As we turn to the New Testament, we see the fulfillment of the promise of the Davidic covenant that a son of David will sit forever on the throne. That promise is fulfilled in the person of Jesus Christ who, according to Paul, "as to his human nature was a descendant of David" (Rom 1:3).

Thus, Luke 1:31-33 records the following blessing upon Mary:

You will be with child and give birth to a son, and you are to give him the name Jesus. He will be great and will be called the Son of the Most High. The Lord God will give him the throne of his father David, and he will reign over the house of Jacob forever; his kingdom will never end. (Lk 1:31-33; compare with Ps 89:3-4)

In summary, then, there are two general grounds for seeing the Psalter as a book which anticipates the coming of Jesus Christ. He is God and he is the son of David. How does this affect our reading of particular psalms?

Singing Hymns to Jesus

Worthy is the Lamb, who was slain,
  to receive power and wealth and wisdom and strength
  and honor and glory and praise!
To him who sits on the throne
  and to the Lamb
be praise and honor and glory and power
      for ever and ever! (Rev 5:12-13)

Jesus is indeed worthy of our praise. As we read the hymns from a New Testament perspective, we lift up our voices to praise Jesus. He is our Savior, our King, our coming judge.

It is appropriate to let the Psalms inform our prayers and it is appropriate to offer our prayers to Jesus. Thus, it is good to sing hymns to Jesus. We may be encouraged as we sing praises to God to know that we don't sing alone. We not only sing

hymns to Jesus, but Jesus sings them with us. This is the meaning of Hebrews 2:12 (citing Ps 22:22):
> I will declare your name to my brothers;
> in the presence of the congregation I will sing your praises.[8]

Singing Laments to Jesus

We have already commented on Jesus taking the laments on his lips as he suffered on our behalf. Now, let us meditate on the laments from another perspective; we may sing our laments to Jesus. The Old Testament saints lifted their petitions and complaints to God. We must do the same. While our prayers shouldn't be consumed with our needs, who else can we turn to for help in our troubles?

When Jesus taught his disciples to pray, he was teaching us (Mt 6:9-12). The prayer (now known to us as the Lord's Prayer) begins with praise:
> Our Father in heaven,
> hallowed be your name,
> your kingdom come,
> your will be done on earth as it is in heaven.

However, this is followed by petition:
> Give us today our daily bread.
> Forgive us our debts,
> as we also have forgiven our debtors.
> And lead us not into temptation,
> but deliver us from the evil one.

Out of fear that our needs and longings will crowd out praise to God, ministers and other Christian leaders emphasize praise in prayers. However, we must be cautious that the pendulum does not swing too far in the other direction so that petition is considered sub-Christian. As we read the laments, we are encouraged and instructed to turn to Jesus with our needs. We can learn from the laments how to be honest with God. The psalmist held nothing back; neither should we.

Singing Thanks to Jesus

After petition was heard and God answered the prayer, the

psalmist returned thanks to God. God had done marvelous things for the psalmist and for the nation of Israel. The psalmist bursts at the seams in gratitude to God.

How much more should we be thankful to God for providing his Son as a sacrifice to atone for our sins? As we read the thanksgiving psalms, let our thanks fly to Jesus who suffered and died for our sakes.

Singing the Psalms of Remembrance to Jesus
The psalmist could look back over the history of his nation and see God's hand at work. He rejoiced as he remembered the exodus, the conquest and the many other times God delivered Israel from distress.

As Christians, we are able to extend redemptive history to its climax beyond the vision of the psalmist. We are able to look back and see God's ultimate redemptive acts that took place on the cross.

The psalmist had a forward-looking perspective. He expected redemption in the future. We too not only look at the present and the past, but anticipate the future. Jesus Christ will return again as judge (as our discussion of Ps 98 in chapter nine will discuss further).

Singing Psalms of Confidence to Jesus
We may sing songs which place our full trust in Jesus because he has promised: "I am with you always, to the very end of the age" (Mt 28:20). Paul spelled out the implications of Christ's abiding presence with us in his well-known words: "For I am convinced that neither death nor life, neither angels nor demons, neither the present nor the future, nor any powers, neither height nor depth, nor anything else in all creation, will be able to separate us from the love of God that is in Christ Jesus our Lord" (Rom 8:38-39).

With such a Savior, we are able to express a confidence as deep as Psalm 23:
Even though I walk through the valley of the
        shadow of death,

> I will fear no evil,
> for you are with me;
> your rod and your staff, they comfort me. (v. 4)

Singing Wisdom Psalms to Jesus

The wisdom psalms call us to be wise, to be righteous, to follow the law of God. As we receive this command, it draws us to Jesus. We learn ever more certainly from the pages of the New Testament that we can't be wise ourselves. We must seek wisdom elsewhere. We find it only in the person of Jesus Christ "in whom are hidden all the treasures of wisdom and knowledge" (Col 2:3).

Conclusion

As we read the Psalms as Christians, two errors need to be avoided. The first is that we neglect a psalm's original setting. Messianic psalms, in an exclusively narrow sense, do not exist.

The second error, though, is to miss the anticipation, the expectation of the Psalms. The New Testament transforms our understanding of the Psalms as we read it in the light of the coming of Jesus Christ.

Suggestions for Psalm Study

18. After interpreting a psalm according to its Old Testament context, consider how the psalm anticipates the coming of Jesus Christ. Ask how the song may be sung to Jesus.

Further Reading

Clowney, E. P. *Preaching and Biblical Theology.* Nutley, N.J.: Presbyterian and Reformed, 1973.

———— , "The Singing Savior." In *Moody Monthly* 79 (1978):40-43.

*Kistemaker, S. *The Psalm Citations in the Epistle to the Hebrew.* Amsterdam, 1961.

Lewis, C. S. "Second Meanings." In *Reflections on the Psalms.* London: Collins, 1961.

5
The Psalms: Mirror of the Soul

In the first chapter we noticed that the appeal of the Psalter is due largely to its ability to speak to the whole person. Usually we read to gain information; we think of it as a cerebral activity. While the Psalms inform us about God and his relationship with people, they do far more. They arouse our emotions, direct our wills and stimulate our imaginations.[1]

We will now look at each of these areas to show that the Psalms are a mirror of our souls. However, we must realize that any such discussion will have two limitations. First, the Psalms are rich beyond measure. It is impossible systematically to exhaust any one of these topics. Our aim is to point the direction, so that we know what to look for later as we study the Psalms for ourselves.

Second, as we discuss how the Psalms appeal to our intellects, wills and emotions, it would be easy to believe that somehow these personality aspects are distinct from one another. This is a false characterization of human personality. All three aspects are intertwined in each one of us.

The Psalms Inform Our Intellect

We often read in order to be informed. We read the front page of the newspaper to learn what events took place the day before. We read the sports page to find out who won last night's big game. We read a textbook on astronomy to discover what stars are made of. We read a book entitled *How to Read the Psalms* to gain information about that book of the Bible.

Most people read to gain factual information. Indeed, one of the Bible's purposes is to give information about God and his dealings with his people. It informs us of the names of individuals and certain events in their lives. It mentions cities which were defeated and buildings which were erected. These facts inform our intellects.

Never, however, does the Bible present us with facts *just* for the purpose of offering information. We are informed by the Bible so that we may know God better.

We don't need to delay over the question of the Psalter's ability to inform us about God and his ways with women and men. It is obvious. Indeed, we have spent the last chapter describing the heart of a theology of the Psalms. But we need to remind ourselves that the Bible as a whole and the Psalms in particular are food for thought. They provide us with information.

The Psalms Arouse Our Emotions

We can't read the Psalms without an emotional response. As the psalmists cry out in joy or grief, they stir us as we identify similar emotions in ourselves.

John Calvin likened the psalms to a mirror:

There is not an emotion of which anyone can be conscious that is not here represented as in a mirror. Or rather, the Holy Spirit has here drawn to the life all the griefs, sorrows, fears, doubts, hopes, cares, perplexities, in short, all the distracting emotions with which the minds of men are wont to be agitated.[2]

In other words, we learn not only about God as we read the Psalms, we learn about ourselves as well. For many of us this can be a frightening prospect.

In one sense, it is fair to say that the Psalms are oriented toward the emotional life of men and women. Emotion permeates the Psalms to such an extent that, as we saw in chapter one, the major types of psalms are identified by their dominant mood: the joy of praise, the sadness of lament and the peace of confidence.

We have already seen more than adequate evidence that praise, confidence and lament are expressed in the Psalter. We can therefore selectively discuss some other emotions.

Reverence. The psalmist often speaks in the presence of God. Accordingly, it is not surprising that he expresses awe toward him:

> But I, by your great mercy,
>> will come into your house;
> in reverence will I bow down toward your
>>> holy temple. (5:7)

The whole of Psalm 8 breathes an atmosphere of awe toward God. This is heightened by the *inclusio* (a repeated phrase at the beginning and end):

> O LORD, our Lord,
>> how majestic is your name in all the earth! (vv. 1, 9)

In the body of the psalm, moreover, the psalmist's awe is motivated by the contemplation of God's creation, particularly his creation of human beings.

Shame. In Psalm 44 the psalmist speaks for the nation. The nation is threatened by enemies, and God is not coming to its aid. "What's wrong?" asks the psalmist in so many words. "We haven't broken the covenant. Please come to save us!"

In the light of these developments, the psalmist expresses his deep sense of shame:

> But now you have rejected and humbled us;
>> you no longer go out with our armies. (v. 9)

> My disgrace is before me all day long,
>> and my face is covered with shame

at the taunts of those who reproach and revile me,
because of the enemy, who is bent on revenge. (v. 15)

Since God hasn't come to Israel's aid when the psalmist thought
he would, he feels a deep sense of embarrassment as he calls
on the name of the Lord.

Fear. Fear is sometimes expressed in a lament, perhaps because the psalmist doubts that God is present.

The psalmist will occasionally admit to fear but is quick to
find peace in God:

When I am afraid,
    I will trust in you. (56:3)

Sadness.

I am worn out from groaning;
    all night long I flood my bed with weeping
    and drench my couch with tears.
My eyes grow weak with sorrow;
    they fail because of all my foes. (6:6-7)

This verse is self-explanatory and expresses an emotion found
in many, many laments. The psalmist is beset with foes and God
is absent. The writer has no recourse but to beseech the Lord
with tears.

Just as the psalmist rarely stays afraid, so he rarely remains
sad. During the course of his prayer, the psalmist is reminded
of God's goodness. Thus, most laments in which there is a
strong note of sadness end with an equally strong note of joy.

Psalm 13 provides a clear example. It is a short song which
begins plaintively:

How long, O LORD?
Will you forget me forever?
    How long will you hide your face from me?
How long must I wrestle with my thoughts
    and every day have sorrow in my heart?
How long will my enemy triumph over me? (vv. 1-2)

In spite of this sad beginning, the psalmist concludes on a
strongly positive note:

But I trust in your unfailing love;

> my heart rejoices in your salvation.
> I will sing to the LORD,
>   for he has been good to me. (v. 5-6)

Anger. Perhaps the most difficult emotion in the Psalter for the Christian to understand is the anger which the psalmist expresses. At times, the anger is so intense that it may rightly be called hate.

> Declare them guilty, O God!
>   Let their intrigues be their downfall. (5:10)
> May his days be few;
>   may another take his place of leadership.
> May his children be fatherless
>   and his wife a widow.
> May his children be wandering beggars;
>   may they be driven from their ruined homes. (109:8-10)

It is hard for Christians who are instructed to turn the other cheek and to love those who hate them (Mt 5:38-48) to understand the curses against the enemies found in the Psalms. This issue will be considered in the exposition of Psalm 69 found in the closing chapter.

Doubt. According to the Old Testament only the fool doubts God's existence:

> The fool says in his heart,
>   "There is no God." (14:1)

For the most part, in the Old Testament the existence of God is not at issue. Few people doubted that God lived. Doubt in Israel was of two kinds. On the one hand, many people in Israel doubted that Yahweh was the one and only God (1 Kings 18). The psalmist never expresses that type of doubt. As a matter of fact, he counters this kind of doubt by showing that the God of the Old Testament is the only God in the universe and has all the power and glory which the pagan gods were thought to possess.

On the other hand, some, even faithful Israelites, questioned the goodness or justice of God. The composer of Psalm 73 shares with us that he had such doubts.

His problem arose as he compared his own life with the lives of evil men. He was surprised to find that evil men were prospering while he was struggling:

For I envied the arrogant
    when I saw the prosperity of the wicked.
They have no struggles;
    their bodies are healthy and strong.
They are free from the burdens common to man;
    they are not plagued by human ills.
Surely in vain have I kept my heart pure;
    in vain have I washed my hands in innocence. (73:3-5, 13)

The song itself was written after the psalmist had regained his composure. He realigned himself with God (v. 17), and matters became clearer to him, so that he could assert in the first verse:

Surely God is good to Israel,
    to those who are pure in heart.

However, for those of us today who sometimes struggle with God's justice as we survey the world and see how evil men and women prosper, we can be encouraged that Psalm 73 was born out of the struggle of doubt and that the psalmist was put back into a right relationship with God.

Love. The psalmist loves the Lord:

I love you, O LORD, my strength. (18:1)
I love the LORD,
    for he heard my voice;
    he heard my cry for mercy. (116:1)

He loves the Lord so much that he expresses his love toward those things associated with him:

I love the house where you live, O LORD,
    the place where your glory dwells. (26:8)

Oh, how I love your law!
    I meditate on it all day long. (119:97)

These examples only begin to scratch the surface of the intense feelings which are expressed in the Psalms. The Psalms speak to us in a wide variety of situations; they arouse our emotions.

As S. G. Meyer, a psychologist, has insightfully put it:
The range of emotional expression often allows the reader
to express his inner life. They assist him in verbalizing what
he heretofore has been unable to communicate. In doing so,
he often crystallizes the nature and identity of his problem.[3]
The Psalms put us in touch with our deepest emotions. As
readers of the Psalms, we can "feel [ourselves] understood and
explained" by them.[4] They also make us sensitive to the emotional struggles of others.

The Psalms teach us that our emotions are grounded in our
faith, our covenant faith. This contradicts our mistaken belief
that emotions are something over which we have no control.

Contrary to this, notice how in the Psalms the composer's
feelings are associated with his relationship to God. When God
is distant, the psalmist is sad, afraid, ashamed, doubtful, even
angry. When God is near, he is happy and secure; he even
expresses his love.

It is simply not true that our emotional life is something over
which we have no control. The Psalms can help us to discipline
our emotions. This does not mean that we should repress our
emotions; far from it, if we follow the example of the psalmist.
The Psalms are an honest expression of emotions. We get a
privileged insight into the negative feelings of the psalmist to
which we can all relate.

In the Psalms, however, the negative always leads to the positive. Doubt leads to trust; anger toward God turns to love;
sadness to joy. But we must remember that the Psalms aren't
magical incantations. It sometimes appears that the psalmist
changed his negative feelings to positive ones in a brief moment, but this isn't how it happened. The Psalms compress time
in such a way that what was a long process appears as a sudden
insight. Honest emotional struggle stands behind the Psalms.

In conclusion, remember that emotions aren't a separate
compartment in our lives. What we know often effects what we
feel; what we feel often determines what we select to know.
Also, feeling often leads to action. With this in mind, we turn
now to see how the Psalms direct our wills.

The Psalms Direct Our Wills

It would be inappropriate here to enter into the controversial debate over the relationship between divine sovereignty and human responsibility, or, in other words, God's will and human free will. Other books can be recommended on that subject.[5]

My point is simple. The Psalms instruct us how we should behave.

This is not to say we can find specific answers to all of our personal and ethical questions in the psalms, but we are exhorted by command and example in the right way to go.

The wisdom psalms: Wisdom psalms deserve special mention as we consider the Psalms as poems which seek to transform our behavior. A major characteristic of these psalms is the contrast which they draw between a righteous lifestyle and a wicked one (Ps 1).

A recurrent formula in these psalms is the blessing:

Blessed is the man
   who does not walk in the counsel of the wicked (1:1)

Blessed is he
   whose transgressions are forgiven,
   whose sins are covered. (32:1)

This is one way in which the Psalms point us in the direction of right behavior. They lead us in the direction of behavior which is approved (blessed) by God.

The wisdom psalms guided the worshiper in the general direction of righteous behavior but did not spell out the specific contents of that righteous behavior. However, they do point outside of themselves to the law. By an intense affirmation of the goodness and benefit of the law of God, the psalmist directed the worshiper to the principles by which a godly person should live life:

Blessed are they whose ways are blameless,
   who walk according to the law of the LORD.
Blessed are they who keep his statutes

and seek him with all their heart.
They do nothing wrong;
    they walk in his ways.
You have laid down precepts that are to be fully obeyed.
Oh, that my ways were steadfast in obeying your decrees!
Then I would not be put to shame
        when I consider all your commands.
I will praise you with an upright heart
        as I learn your righteous laws.
I will obey your decrees;
    do not utterly forsake me. (119:1-8)

Directing our wills by example. The Psalms place before us examples of righteous behavior particularly in the area of worship. We not only learn more about the object of our worship, God, but also that we should worship and how we should worship.

The psalmist teaches us how we should behave toward God by example. P. B. Power, a student of the Psalms in the middle of the nineteenth century, wrote an interesting book with the title *The 'I Wills' of the Psalms* (see further reading at the end of the chapter). He studied passages of the Psalms in which the psalmist made an affirmation of a course of behavior which he will follow. A few examples include:

I will give thanks to the LORD because of his righteousness (Ps 7:17—we should thank God)

Even though I walk through the valley of the shadow
        of death,
I will fear no evil (Ps 23:4—we should trust God)

I will tell of all your wonders. (Ps 9:1—we should witness to God's salvation)

Then I will teach transgressors your ways,
    and sinners will turn back to you. (Ps. 51:13—we should witness to God's law)

In the day of my trouble I will call to you (Ps 86:7—we should pray when we are in trouble)

I will run in the path of your commands (Ps 119:32—we
should be obedient)

These are just a few of the many affirmations which the psalmist makes in the course of his prayers. From them we can learn
how we should act as well.

But it is not just from these "I wills" of the psalms that we
learn. We must look at the whole of each psalm in its context
to glean what God wants us to emulate.

Directing our wills by command. The setting of most of the
Psalms, as we have argued in chapter two, is in formal worship.
A congregation's presence is frequently assumed.

Accordingly, we find the worship leader frequently exhorting
the people to worship the Lord. As we study these commands
in the Psalms, we should be stirred from the common attitude
which American Christians take toward worship.

Worship in many churches is a spectator sport. If we listen
to the commands of the psalmist, our worship will radically
change. It will become both *communal* and *enthusiastic:*

Clap your hands, all you nations;
    shout to God with cries of joy. (47:1)

Ascribe to the LORD, O mighty ones,
    ascribe to the LORD glory and strength.
Ascribe to the LORD the glory due his name;
    worship the LORD in the splendor of his holiness.
    (29:1-2)

Praise the LORD, O my soul;
    all my inmost being, praise his holy name.
Praise the LORD, O my soul,
    and forget not all his benefits (103:1-2)

The Psalms were born from life struggles, and they speak to

people who struggle today. They also arose from people who had experienced liberation from struggle, and so we find expression to our joy when God liberates us from oppression.

Conclusion
As we read a psalm, we learn about God and his care for us. We learn about ourselves as well. We understand our situation better because the whole gamut of human experience is expressed in the Psalter. As David Hubbard put it, the Psalms speak to all seasons of our souls.[6]

Our intellect is informed, our emotions are refined, and our wills are directed. What further motivation do we need to spend time reading and meditating on the Psalms?

Suggestions for Psalm Study
19. As you read a psalm, explore the psalmist's emotional expression.
20. Ask yourself: How can I learn from the psalmist's example?

Further Reading
Unfortunately, there is not much available on this aspect of the Psalms.
Power, P. B. *The 'I Wills' of the Psalms.* 1858. Reprint. Carlisle, Pa.: Banner of Truth, 1985.

Part II
The Art
of the Psalms

6
Old
Testament
Poetry

It's easy to recognize that the Psalms are poetry! All one has to do is open the Bible to the book of Psalms, and then turn to Leviticus and notice the contrast. We don't even need to read a word. Short, almost equal lines make up the Psalms (leaving a lot of white space on the pages), while the book of Leviticus is clearly prose and our English translations present it as such. The sentences are long and print fills the page. The breaks are at paragraphs and these are indented.

Once we start reading, other characteristics spring out. Compare Leviticus 1 and Psalm 1. Notice the repetition in the lines of the psalm:

> his delight is in the law of the LORD,
>   and on his law he meditates day and night. (v. 2)

> Therefore the wicked will not stand in the judgment,
>   nor sinners in the assembly of the righteous. (v. 5)

Notice too the abundance of metaphors or images which the psalmist uses to communicate his message: "the seat of mockers" (v. 1), "he is like a tree planted by streams of water" (v. 3) and the wicked are "like chaff" (v. 4). Leviticus 1, on the other hand, has a minimum of repetition between lines and a lack of images. The language is much closer to everyday conversational English.

The psalms are clearly poetic, and indeed poetry makes up much of the Old Testament. Most English versions of the Bible print the poetic portions in a distinctive way. By simply leafing through the Bible, we can get a quick feel for how much of the Old Testament is poetry.

The whole of the Psalms, the books of Job, Song of Solomon, Lamentations, Proverbs, most of Ecclesiastes, most of the prophets (there are large exceptions in Jeremiah, Daniel, Jonah) and even sections of the historical books (see Gen 49; Ex 15; Judges 5; 2 Sam 22; and many others) are poetry. Thus, the next three chapters of this book have ramifications for our reading of a good portion of the Old Testament. We will concentrate, however, on the subject of this book, Psalms.

Why Poetry?

The fact that the Psalms and so much of the rest of the Old Testament are in poetic form leads us to a question. Why do we find so much poetry? If the Bible reveals the truth concerning God, people and the world, why isn't that truth communicated to us in a straightforward prose style?

Consider science with its concern to discover and communicate truths about the universe. Do scientists present their conclusions in poetic form? Of course not. They use the most precise and unambiguous language they can devise, reducing it to mathematical formulas if possible. Why then is there poetry in the Bible?

Furthermore, poetry is hard to read. This is true not only for Hebrew poetry, but for English poetry as well. Sometimes it seems as if the poets are purposefully trying to elude our understanding! Poetry takes more effort to interpret than prose. Here is an example from the opening lines of Sir Philip Sidney's "Astrophel and Stella":

Loving in truth, and fain in verse my love to show,
That she, dear she, might take some pleasure of my pain,
Pleasure might cause her read, reading might make her
                                                    know,
knowledge might pity win, and pity grace obtain,
I sought fit words to paint the blackest face of woe:
Studying inventions fine, her wits to entertain,
Oft turning others' leaves, to see if thence would flow
Some fresh and fruitful showers upon my sunburn'd brain.[1]

If Sidney wanted to communicate his heartfelt feelings to his love, why didn't he send flowers with the simple statement "I love you"?

On one level, this question (why there is so much poetry in the Bible) cannot be answered. God stands behind the form and content of the Bible, and we cannot read God's mind on such matters. However, on the basis of our understanding of how poetry functions and of our own experience with reading poetry, we can offer an answer.

Poems appeal to the whole person in a way that prose does not. Listen to a part of the prose account of the deliverance from the Red Sea (recorded in Ex 14:26-31).

Then the LORD said to Moses, "Stretch out your hand over the sea so that the waters may flow back over the Egyptians and their chariots and horsemen."

Moses stretched out his hand over the sea, and at daybreak the sea went back to its place. The Egyptians were fleeing toward it, and the LORD swept them into the sea. The water flowed back and covered the chariots and horsemen—the entire army of Pharaoh that had followed the Israelites into the sea. Not one of them survived.

But the Israelites went through the sea on dry ground, with a wall of water on their right and on their left. That day the LORD saved Israel from the hands of the Egyptians, and Israel saw the Egyptians lying dead on the shore. And when the Israelites saw the great power the LORD displayed against the Egyptians, the people feared the LORD and put their trust in him and in Moses his servant.

It's an exciting story, but now read Exodus 15:

I will sing to the LORD,
    for he is highly exalted.
The horse and its rider he has hurled into the sea.
The LORD is my strength and my song;
    he has become my salvation.
He is my God, and I will praise him.
    my father's God, and I will exalt him.
The LORD is a warrior,
    the LORD is his name.
Pharaoh's chariots and his army he has hurled into the sea.
The best of Pharaoh's officers are drowned in the Red Sea.
The deep waters have covered them;
    they sank to the depths like a stone. (vv. 1-5)

Notice the difference? If we read the story with any feeling at all, we can't help but be caught up in the excitement of the Israelites themselves in a way that the prose account fails to accomplish.

This is not to demean the prose account of the deliverance from the Red Sea, only to suggest that it serves a different function than the poetic version. For one thing we gain more historical information from the prose account in Exodus 14 than we do from the poetic one in Exodus 15.

The point is that poetry appeals more directly to the whole person than prose does. It stimulates our imaginations, arouses our emotions, feeds our intellects and addresses our wills. Perhaps this is why poetry is the preferred mode of communication of the prophets, whose purpose depends on capturing the attention of their listeners and persuading them their message is urgent.

More than this, poetry is pleasurable. It is attractive to read and even more so to read aloud (or sing). This is not to deny that some prose sections are also highly stylized, but poetry is more consistently literary.[2]

Nevertheless, poetry is difficult to interpret. This is particularly true when the poetry is thousands of years old and written in the context of a foreign culture. Poetry is written in different ways in different cultures and at different times, although there are some common elements. We therefore need to learn "how poetry works" in the Old Testament. In this way we can better understand the Psalms and the other poetic portions of the Old Testament.

What Is Poetry?

What characterizes poetry in the Old Testament? What makes it different from the prose sections? This is the question which we will answer briefly before launching into a longer discussion in the following chapters.

We have seen how recognizable poetic portions of the Bible are in most English translations because the text is not written in paragraphs but in short lines of roughly equal lengths. Of course, this is not the form in which the psalms have come down to us from the Hebrew scribes; it is the decision of modern interpreters and translators to present the text in this format. It is a good decision, but what leads them and us to read these passages as poetry rather than prose?

Poetry is distinguished from prose in the Old Testament, not by one, but by a whole host of characteristics. These are important for us to understand, so that we can properly interpret a psalm or any other poem. Here we will mention the traits of Hebrew poetry; further discussion follows. Each of these traits, while appearing occasionally in prose, occur frequently and together in poetry.

The single most common characteristic of Hebrew poetry is repetition, usually called *parallelism*.

Notice, for instance, the repetition of the first and second parts of Psalm 20:1:

May the LORD answer you when you are in distress;
    may the name of the God of Jacob protect you.

The second part is parallel with the first. Reading through the next four verses, we notice that this parallelism continues.

The psalm at first glance seems needlessly repetitive to us, and yet we recognize the psalm's beauty and power. How does this repetition enhance the poem's beauty and power? How are we to understand it? Parallelism is the subject of chapter seven.

Those acquainted with either classical (Greek and Roman) or English poetry, will be aware that the predominant trait of these poetic traditions is meter. Meter is a set, patterned rhythm. Many scholars have sought meter in Hebrew poetry but to no avail. Many commentaries, however, use meter in interpreting the Psalms, and so a brief comment on meter will be added to the next chapter.

A second major characteristic of Hebrew poetry is imagery. Granted, you can find images in the prose sections of the Old Testament as well, but not to the same extent as that found in poetry. Psalm 23 speaks of God as our shepherd. Psalm 29 pictures God as the force in the storm and as the one enthroned over the sea. Proverbs 8 described God's wisdom as a virtuous woman. Hundreds of images flash before our eyes as we read poetry. How do we recognize images so as to avoid interpreting something literally which should be taken figuratively? Why are images so frequent in poetry, particularly the Psalms? Chapter eight will address questions like these.

In the final analysis, what can we say distinguishes Hebrew poetry from prose? Certainly no one characteristic or group of characteristics clearly defines poetry. As I said before, parallelism occurs in prose occasionally, as does imagery. However, in those sections we recognize as poetry we find a heightened and intensified use of parallelism and imagery. The sentences are short and of approximately equal length. Poetry, in a word, is distinguishable from prose in that it is distanced from everyday language. Prose has a close resemblance to the way in which we talk every day to our friends, relatives and acquaintances. Poetry, by contrast, is an artificial language.

So, for the next two chapters, our goal is to come to a better understanding of how to read Hebrew poetry in general and the Psalms in particular. The examples, however, will be taken mainly from the Psalms.

7
Understanding Parallelism

O LORD, do not rebuke me in your anger
 or discipline me in your wrath.
Be merciful to me, LORD, for I am faint;
 O LORD, heal me, for my bones are in agony. (6:1-2)
Reading these opening verses of Psalm 6, we are struck by the
amount of repetition within the lines. In the first verse, the
verbs "rebuke" and "discipline" are parallel as are the prepositional
phrases which follow, "in your anger" and "in your
wrath." In the second verse the psalmist twice calls on the Lord.
He beseeches the Lord to "be merciful" and to "heal" him, and
in both lines a reason is given, "for . . ."

These two lines are clear instances of parallelism. Parallelism
refers to the correspondence which occurs between the phrases
of a poetic line. This correspondence, as we will see, may take
many forms, but even the novice reader of Old Testament poetry
can recognize a resemblance between phrases in a line.

Before we attempt to go any further in discussing how the
individual units of a psalm "work," it will be helpful to introduce
some terminology with which to describe the individual
units.

One complete parallelism we will call a *line*. Each line, so defined, will contain two, sometimes three, and rarely four or more *poetic phrases*. The first line of Psalm 2 may serve as an example.

Why do the nations conspire and the peoples plot in vain?

This line may clearly be divided into two *phrases:* the first, "Why do the nations conspire"; the second, "and the peoples plot in vain." Since there are two phrases in this poetic line, it is often called a *bicolon*. When there are three phrases, the line is referred to as a *tricolon*. Monocola (poetic lines with only one phrase) are also well attested. We will occasionally mark the first colon of a line as *A;* the second, *B;* the third, *C;* and so forth. This is simply for ease of reference.

Hebrew poetry uses a concise, rich language. It is meant to be read slowly and carefully in order to receive the full impact of the message of the Psalms. Reading a psalm closely, one needs a reading strategy. How should we understand these repetitions—the relationship between phrases (or cola) in a line of Hebrew poetry?

There are three possibilities, each of which has been advocated at some point in church history.

1. A ≠ B: *The early view.* This approach to parallelism may be called the "*A* does not equal *B*" approach. I call it the early view because it was a dominant view for reading poetry before about A.D. 1750. This approach is partially correct. As a matter of fact, it will help us recover one of the essential elements of Old Testament poetry. Alone, however, it leads to real problems.

For instance, notice the way in which some early rabbis interpreted Genesis 21:1.

Now the LORD was gracious to Sarah as he had said,
    and the LORD did for Sarah what he had promised.

This verse is from a prose context, but there is obvious parallelism between the two phrases. The clear reference of the phrases in this line is to the promise of God that the aged and barren Sarah would give birth to a child. However, early rabbinic exegetes, approaching the term from an "*A* does not equal *B*" perspective, expended their energy speculating first about what the Lord had said to Sarah and second about what he had promised her. For instance, Rabbi Yehuda said that the birth of a son was fulfillment of what God *said*, while the blessing of milk with which she nursed her son was a fulfillment of what he *promised*.[1]

You get the picture. On the principle that God doesn't waste words, this approach denies the parallelism and looks for two *different* meanings. This leads to incredible stretching of the meaning of the line as in the case of Yehuda's interpretation of Genesis 21:1.

2. A = B: *The traditional approach.* Around A.D. 1750, Robert Lowth of Oxford, England, revolutionized our understanding of parallelism.[2] He clearly defined how parallelism worked and described what he felt were the three major types of parallelism. If you read a textbook on Old Testament poetry, it is highly likely that the view presented will be that of Lowth, thus the title "traditional" approach.

Lowth coined the term *parallelism* and went on to define it as "when equals refer to equals, and opposites to opposites."[3] In short, the *A* phrase equals the *B* phrase. Lowth reversed the way most people had been reading Old Testament poetry during the eighteenth century and before.

Take a look again at the two verses from Psalm 6 at the beginning of the chapter. Lowth and his modern followers would interpret each verse as saying the same thing twice, simply using different words. The goal of interpretation, therefore, is to reduce the two poetic phrases into one prose sentence. For verse 1, this might be something like "Lord, don't punish me when you are angry with me," and for verse 2, "Help me, Lord, when I'm hurting."

Lowth's view was a definite step forward in our understanding how parallelism works. However, such an approach flattens out the poetic line. That this approach is only found in contemporary handbooks on the Psalms may be seen in reference to C. S. Lewis who errs by defining parallelism as "the practice of saying the same thing twice in different words."[4]

3. A, *what's more* B: *The proper approach.*[5] As with most good

things, the truth is somewhere between the two extremes! The "early view" errs by overemphasizing the difference between the two phrases within a bicolon. The "traditional view" over-emphasizes the similarity or repetition.

As we read the lines of Hebrew poetry carefully, we see that the second phrase is related in meaning to the first phrase. However—and this is important—it *always* carries forward the thought found in the first phrase in some way. This insight into the nature of parallelism has come to the attention of scholars through the work of James Kugel (see suggested reading at the end of the chapter). It is a simple insight, but causes a radical shift in how one reads poetry.

Let's turn back to Psalm 6. How does the second phrase go beyond the first here?

In Psalm 6:1 the psalmist pleads with the Lord not to rebuke him. A rebuke is a reprimand in words. In the second part of verse 1, the psalmist pleads with God not to discipline him. This is a more serious matter, stepping beyond mere words to action.

In 6:2 we again find the progression from words to action. The psalmist begs the Lord in the first place to be merciful to him. Then in the second part he pleads with God actually to heal him (the psalm is a plea to God by someone who is very ill).

Also in verse 2, two reasons are given to God by the psalmist. These are found in the second part of both phrases, following the *for*. The second is a much stronger expression of the psalmist's pain than the first, *fainting* followed by *agony*.

This third approach *(A, what's more B)* is the one we will follow in reading the poetry of the Psalms. It incorporates the good insights of the first two, "the early" and "the traditional" approaches.

Of course, there are different purposes to the Psalms and different ways we may want to read them. Most of the time we should simply sit down and read them at a normal reading rate. At other times we may want to do a close study of the psalm, pausing after each line to ask how the phrases relate to one another and what the line as a whole means.

The Categories of Parallelism

Besides modifying his contemporaries' understanding of parallelism, Robert Lowth identified three major types of parallelism. These three categories have become standard ways of describing the poetic line.

1. Synonymous parallelism. Synonymous parallelism occurs the most frequently and is the best known of the three categories. Synonymous parallelism, according to most interpreters, is the repetition of the same thought in two different phrases using two different, yet closely related, sets of words. Psalm 2 is, with only minor exceptions, constructed out of synonymous lines.

Why do the nations conspire
    and the peoples plot in vain?
The kings of the earth take their stand
    and the rulers gather together
against the LORD
    and against his Anointed One.
"Let us break their chains," they say,
    "and throw off their fetters."

Each part of the first phrase is paralleled by a near synonym in the second.

2. Antithetic parallelism. The label *antithetic parallelism* may give the mistaken impression that this category of parallelism is the opposite of synonymous parallelism. On the contrary, it functions similarly. Both, according to Lowth, state the same thought twice using different terms.

The label could lead you to the misunderstanding that the phrases are stating two contrary propositions. Lowth, however, meant that, just as in synonymous parallelism, the same thought is expressed, but this time using antonyms (a word whose meaning is the opposite of another word: skinny/fat; kind/mean) instead of synonyms. In other words, the same thought is expressed, but expressed from two different and often opposite perspectives.

The book of Proverbs is full of antithetical parallelism. After all, one of the main themes of the book is to contrast the traits, lifestyles and rewards of two opposite classes of people—the wicked and the righteous, the foolish and the wise.

> A wise son brings joy to his father,
> but a foolish son grief to his mother. (Prov 10:1)

There are three pairs of opposites in this verse: wise son vs. foolish, joy vs. grief and mother vs. father. But observe that the same point is being made from two polar extremes.

3. Synthetic parallelism. Lowth concluded his description of the types of parallelism with a third category, synthetic parallelism. Synthetic parallelism labels those lines in which the second phrase completes or supplements the first. There is little positive to be said in favor of retaining this category. As a matter of fact, it is likely that synthetic lines are not parallel at all. The label has been used by some scholars as a "catchall" for those lines which are neither synonymous nor antithetic. The following verses are representative of what is meant by synthetic parallelism.

> I have installed my King
> on Zion, my holy hill. (2:6)

> When the LORD brought back the captives to Zion,
> we were like men who dreamed. (126:1)

Synthetic parallelism is mentioned here only because most textbooks and many commentaries use the term, so you should know what it is and why it is not a very helpful classification.

Synonymous, antithetic and synthetic parallelisms are the basic building blocks of a traditional approach to classifying relationships between phrases in poetic lines. It is not surprising to find that the tendency of scholarship has been to increase the number of categories. Here are a few of the newer categories.

4. Emblematic parallelism. Emblematic parallelism explicitly draws an analogy. In other words, one of the phrases in an emblematic line will use a word of comparison *(like, as)* in order to bring together two thoughts from different spheres of life to illumine a theological or didactic teaching.

As the deer pants for streams of water,
   so my soul pants for you, O God. (42:1)

Like a fluttering sparrow or a darting swallow,
   an undeserved curse does not come to rest. (Prov 26:2)

5. Repetitive parallelism. We could call this type of parallelism stepladder, staircase or climactic parallelism. As these names imply, repetitive parallelism begins with a statement in the first phrase which is partially repeated in the second but carried further than it would be in synonymous parallelism. Psalm 29 provides a good example.
   Ascribe to the LORD, O mighty ones,
      ascribe to the LORD glory and strength.
         Ascribe to the LORD the glory due his name;
            worship the LORD in the splendor of his holiness.
            (29:1)

6. Pivot pattern. Though it sounds like a basketball play, the pivot pattern is actually a highly sophisticated type of parallelism. In this type of parallelism there is a word or clause which stands in the middle of the poetic line and which can and should be read with both the *A* and *B* phrases.
   A The LORD has made his salvation known
      to the nations
   B and revealed his righteousness. (Ps 98:2, translation mine)
Many English translations obscure this type of parallelism, but in the Hebrew the phrase "to the nations" occurs between the *A* and the *B* phrases. *To the nations* should be read with both the first and the last phrases. According to Psalm 98, the Lord has made his salvation known to the nations, and he has revealed his righteousness to the nations.

7. Chiasm. Perhaps the most interesting and certainly one of the most frequently encountered categories of parallelism is the chiasm. The name *chiasm* comes from the name for the Greek letter *chi* which is in the form of two crossing lines (a large *X*). This is appropriate because, when diagrammed, a simple chiastic line will take the form of an *X*:

Examples of chiastic lines in Old Testament poetry are found in Psalm 1:

> Blessed is the man who does not walk in the
>   counsel of the wicked
> and in the way of sinners he does not stand.
>   (v. 1, translation mine)

> For the LORD watches over the way of the righteous
>   but the way of the wicked will perish. (v. 6)

Chiasm may also be discovered on a higher structural level in the Psalms. Psalm 2, for instance, breaks down into four stanzas arranged according to chiasm. The first (vv. 1-3) and the last (vv. 10-12) stanzas both refer to the kings of the earth and the action that takes place on the earth. The two middle stanzas (vv. 4-6 and 7-9) narrate heavenly activities. The result is a chiastic pattern for the poem as a whole:

earth heaven
heaven earth

These six types of parallelism are frequently found in poetry, but you must be careful how you use them. We must always bear in mind that, while the second phrase will always progress the thought of the first, it may do so in a vast number of ways. The relationship between A and B can't be limited to these six categories, but they are a start.[6] In other words, they represent six frequent ways in which A is more than B.

Turn to Psalm 23 and read the whole poem. The psalm begins with the well-known and beloved line:

The LORD is my shepherd, I shall not be in want. (v. 1)

Right away we are thrown into a bit of a quandary if we restrict ourselves to the six major categories above. Many traditional interpreters would simply call this line "synthetic" parallelism and leave it at that, but we've seen that synthetic parallelism is a kind of catchall category with no real significance.

Looking closely at the line, we observe a cause-effect relationship between its first and second parts. The meaning of the line, accordingly, is: Because the Lord is my shepherd, therefore I shall not be in want. This verse stands at the head of the whole psalm and sets the tone for what follows.

The next two verses (five phrases) go together:

> He makes me lie down in green pastures,
>> he leads me beside quiet waters,
>> he restores my soul.
> He guides me in paths of righteousness
>> for his name's sake. (vv. 2-3)

The shepherd's care for his sheep unites these five phrases. Four actions are given, one in each phrase, carrying forward the image of God as shepherd and his people as the flock of his pasture. Occasionally the imagery is broken through, hinting to the reader how to apply the imagery to reality. Sheep don't, for instance, follow paths of "righteousness." They don't have souls which need restoration.

Examining the relationship between these five phrases, the reader notices that, while there is similarity between them, there is also a gradual progression. This progression is especially clear between the first, second and third phrases. We move from lying down to leading; then finally to guiding. There is an intensification from phrase to phrase.

The last clause, *for his name's sake,* has no parallel in the psalm and as a result clearly stands apart from the other phrase. Divergence from a set pattern is a way by which Hebrew poets emphasized a line.

Verse 4 is a clear example of a pivot pattern:

> Even though I walk through the valley of the shadow of death,
>> I will fear no evil,
>> for you are with me.

The middle clause should be read with both the first and last phrase of the line. The result is two complete lines which share the clause "I will fear no evil."

Even though I walk through the valley of the shadow of death,

I will fear no evil.

I will fear no evil, for you are with me.

The last line in the first stanza, "your rod and your staff, they comfort me," continues the last thought of the preceding line. The rod and the staff represent the presence of the shepherd since they are the tools of his trade, so to speak (as a scepter represents a king). The last phrase of the previous line had emphasized that God was with him. Because God is present the psalmist is comforted.

Psalm 3:1-4

A O LORD, how many are my foes!

B How many rise up against me!

C Many are saying of me, "God will not deliver him."

D But you are a shield around me, O LORD,

E you bestow glory on me and lift up my head.

F To the LORD I cry aloud, and he answers me from
        his holy hill. (3:1-4)

The first three phrases (A, B and C) are united by the mention of a large number of enemies—the "many." But once again, the phrases are not strictly synonymous or making the same statement three times.

We can easily see that each phrase progresses the thought appreciably. The first phrase (A) is an expression of the vast number of the psalmist's foes. The second phrase (B) carries the thought further by informing the listener that these foes are attacking him. Last, the third phrase (C) gets more specific concerning the many foes by quoting their taunts against the psalmist. Thus in these first three phrases (A, B and C), we have (1) a description of the numerous foes, (2) an assertion of their active hostility toward the psalmist, and (3) a word from the foes.

The second line (a tricolon as well) is related to the first. Here the three phrases are united by the mention of the Lord and contain the same threefold progression as the first poetic line.

The first phrase *(D)* describes the Lord as a protector; the second phrase *(E)* states the Lord's active intervention for his people; and the third phrase *(F)* mentions a word from the Lord.

As opposed to the word from the foes *(C)*, the word from the Lord is only mentioned and not quoted. Nevertheless, the Lord's reply to the psalmist is a fitting contrast to the word from the foes, who claim that God will not help the psalmist.

Grammatical Parallelism

As we have seen, parallelism has to do with similarities and differences between phrases within a line. The similarities cause us to read two phrases together. The variation found in the second phrase carries the meaning of the psalm forward.

Thus far, this chapter has really concentrated on only one type of parallelism, *semantic* parallelism. (Semantics has to do with the meaning of words.)

A second important type of parallelism is called *grammatical* parallelism. Grammatical parallelism charts the similarities and differences between the parts of speech used in related phrases (morphology) and also in the word order (syntax).

Serious study of grammatical parallelism, however, requires a knowledge of Hebrew and is beyond the scope of this book. Interested readers should read the book by Adele Berlin mentioned at the end of the chapter.

An example to be looked at briefly is Psalm 2:5. Here is my own translation which reflects the word order of the Hebrew:

Then he rebukes them in his anger
    and in his wrath he terrifies them.

The semantic parallelism is obvious. The verbs are *rebuke* and *terrify* each time with *them* as a direct object. *Anger* and *wrath* are also parallel in meaning.

The grammatical parallelism is obvious as well. The similarity between these two phrases is that each has a verb, a direct object and a prepositional phrase. They parallel each other and cause us to read these phrases together as a single line.

However, notice the subtle difference as well. The word order in each is different:

Verb—direct object—prepositional phrase

Prepositional phrase—verb—direct object

As with semantic parallelism, the grammatical similarity within a poetic line causes us to link its two phrases together. The slight variations in grammar avoid the possibility of monotony.

Ellipsis

There is one other important fact about parallelism that must be pointed out before we proceed to some more extensive examples. Most of the poetic lines we've encountered so far have been *complete parallelism*. In other words, each part of the first phrase is paralleled in the second.

> Let them exalt him in the assembly of the people
> and praise him in the council of the elders. (107:32)

Frequently, however, the second phrase will omit a part of the first clause with the understanding that the omitted part of the first clause is to be read into the second clause. Usually it is the verb which is omitted:

> You have put me in the lowest pit,
> in the darkest depths. (88:6)

The verb is missing in the second phrase, but of course we are to understand the sense of the second phrase as:

> (You have put me) in the darkest depths.

This poetic device is called ellipsis. The effect of ellipsis is to bind two phrases more closely together. There is no question as to whether the two phrases go together in a single line. A further effect, however, is economy of expression. You will come across ellipsis frequently in your reading of the Psalms and the other poetical portions of Scripture.

Secondary Poetic Devices

Besides parallelism (described in this chapter) and imagery (to be described in the next chapter), a number of other ornamental devices appear in Hebrew poetry. While parallelism and imagery are very frequent in Old Testament poetry, the others are secondary in that they appear less regularly.

Ancient Hebrew poets "beautified" and enhanced their poetic creations in many different ways. Only a few of the more interesting and more noticeable types can be described here. Interested readers will want to consult some of the more advanced books on the subject recommended at the end of the chapter (particularly the book by W. G. E. Watson).

Inclusio. The *inclusio* is associated with parallelism in that it involves repetition in a poem in a way which binds its parts together. In this case, however, it is not repetition between phrases in a line which is at issue but rather a repetition which opens and closes a poem. An obvious instance of *inclusio* is found in Psalm 8. Here we encounter strict repetition in the opening and closing verses. Both verse 1 and verse 9 read:

O LORD, our Lord, how majestic is your name in all the earth!

An *inclusio* gives the reader of the psalm a sense of closure, a sense of having read a complete poem. It imparts to the psalm a sense of unity, and perhaps most important, it sets the mood for the whole psalm. In the case of Psalm 8, it promotes an attitude of awe toward God.

Another simple example of *inclusio* occurs in Psalm 106. This psalm opens and closes with the Hebrew phrase *Hallelu Yah,* translated *Praise the LORD!*

A more complicated *inclusio* appears in Psalm 69. The repetition here is not between the first and last verses, but rather between the first and second to last verses. Also, the repetition is between two words which, though from the same root, actually are slightly different forms in the Hebrew.

Save me, O God (v. 1)

for God *will save* Zion. (v. 35)

Acrostic poetry. One of the more interesting twists on the poetic line in the Old Testament is the so-called acrostic poem. An acrostic is a poem in which the first letter of each line, taken together, forms a recognizable pattern. While some poems from ancient times (such as some Babylonian poems) spell out the name of the scribe who copied the text, or perhaps some hidden message, the examples found in the Old Testament all follow the order of the Hebrew alphabet.

The most famous acrostic in the Bible is the "Giant Psalm," Psalm 119. Here each stanza has eight lines which begin with the same letter of the alphabet. Thus the first eight verses of Psalm 119 begin with words which have as their initial letter the *aleph* (equivalent to our letter *A*). This pattern continues through the next twenty stanzas. Other psalms devote just one line or a single phrase to a letter. Among the acrostic psalms are Psalms 9, 10, 25, 34, 37, 111, 112, 119, 145.

No one is certain what function acrostics serve. They may be a formal way of reflecting their trust that God gave order to his creation. More likely they are a device to aid memorization or were simply aesthetically pleasing to ancient Israelite poets. Perhaps the additional word-choice restrictions made composition more difficult and thus made the end product all the more exciting to produce and to read.

Meter

Meter is a patterned rhythm that structures a whole poem. Most English and classical poems are structured by meter, and so many, many biblical scholars have felt that Hebrew poetry had to have it as well. However, recent research has concluded that the psalms are not metrical. (If you are interested in why this is the case, read my article on meter listed in the bibliography.)

It wouldn't even have been necessary to mention meter in this book, except that many scholars and commentaries use meter as a criterion for adding or subtracting words or phrases from the individual psalms. I believe it is best, accordingly, to ignore any interpretation based on meter.

Suggestions for Psalm Study

21. Read the psalm slowly. Examine the relationship between the lines for similarities and differences.
22. On the basis of these similarities and differences, divide the lines into phrases (bicola and tricola).

23. When reading a poetic line, ask how the second phrase carries forward the thought of the first.

24. Don't force the similarities. Not every phrase in a poem will be parallel with another. Some will be more parallel than others.

25. The above six categories (synthetic parallelism is excluded) are *rough* guides to discovering the relationship between the two phrases of a poetic line.

Exercises

1. Read Psalm 2 and identify the separate poetic lines. Identify the phrases within these lines and label them as mono-, bi-or tricola.

2. Analyze Psalm 46. Read it slowly. Group together the phrases and lines which resemble one another into bicola and tricola. Analyze the relationship between the lines.

3. Do you see any ellipsis in Psalm 47?

4. Identify the type of parallelism found in the following passages according to the six traditional categories of parallelism (synonymous, antithetical, emblematic, repetitive, pivot, chiastic):

a.   At the presence of the LORD,
     tremble, O earth,
     at the presence of the God of Jacob. (114:7,
          translation mine)

b.   I will instruct you and teach you in the way you should go;
     I will counsel you and watch over you. (32:8)

c.   I have seen a wicked and ruthless man
     flourishing like a green tree in its native soil (37:35).

d.   The waters saw you, O God,
     the waters saw you and writhed;
     the very depths were convulsed. (77:16)

e.   O LORD, before you lie open all of my longings;
     my sighing is not hidden from you (38:9,
          translation mine)

110

Further Reading

Alter, Robert. *The Art of Biblical Poetry.* New York: Basic Books, 1985.

Barfield, Owen. *Poetic Diction.* Middletown, Conn.: Wesleyan University Press, 1973.

*Berlin, Adele. *The Dynamics of Biblical Parallelism.* Bloomington: Indiana University Press, 1985.

*Fraser, G. S. *Metre, Rhyme and Free Verse.* Critical Idiom 8. London: Methuen, 1970.

Geller, S. A. *Parallelism in Early Biblical Poetry.* Harvard Semitic Monographs 20. Missoula, Mont.: Scholars Press, 1979.

Kugel, James. *The Idea of Biblical Poetry.* New Haven: Yale University Press, 1981.

*Longman, Tremper, III. "A Critique of Two Recent Metrical Systems." In *Biblica* 63 (1982):230-54.

*O'Connor, Michael. *Hebrew Verse Structure.* Winona Lake, Ind.: Eisenbrauns, 1980.

Watson, W. G. E. *Classical Hebrews Poetry.* JSOTS 26. Sheffield: JSOT Press, 1984.

8
Imagery
in the
Psalms

The Psalms are rich with images. Think for a moment about the many ways in which God is described in the Psalms. He is a shield, a fortress, a rock, a storm cloud, a shepherd, a warrior, an archer, a chariot rider, a king and so much more. Unless we understand how imagery works, we will miss much of the message of the psalms.

Of course, like parallelism, imagery is something we meet throughout the Bible and not just in the Psalter. However, images occur more frequently in poetry than in prose portions of the Bible.

What Is an Image?

As we read a poem, pictures form in our minds. Read Psalm 113 slowly:

¹Praise the LORD.

   Praise, O servants of the LORD,
      praise the name of the LORD.
²Let the name of the LORD be praised,
   both now and forevermore.
³From the rising of the sun to the place where it sets,

the name of the LORD is to be praised.
⁴The LORD is exalted over all the nations,
   his glory above the heavens.
⁵Who is like the LORD our God,
   the One who sits enthroned on high,
      ⁶who stoops down to look on the heavens and the earth?
⁷He raises the poor from the dust
   and lifts the needy from the ash heap
⁸he seats them with princes,
   with the princes of their people.
⁹He settles the barren woman in her home
   as a happy mother of children.
Praise the LORD.

This psalm, by the way, is closely related to the song which Hannah sings when she is praising the Lord for the birth of Samuel (1 Sam 2:1-10). She may have had Psalm 113 in mind as she was composing her own song of praise. The psalm is remarkably similar to Mary's song in Luke 1:46-53 as well.

As you reach the fourth verse, you get a picture of God seated on a magnificent throne. Indeed his throne is so high that he looks down not only to see the earth but also heaven!

The next few verses evoke an image which emphasizes God's compassion for men and women. He is indeed exalted on high, but he also stoops down to take care of the poor and the needy. In verses 6 and 7 the picture of God lifting the poor and leading them to thrones comes to mind.

In short, the psalm gives us a clear picture. We see, on the one hand, God enthroned in heaven; on the other, God helping the poor.

Now read Psalm 114 closely:

¹When Israel came out of Egypt,
   the house of Jacob from a people of foreign tongue,
²Judah became God's sanctuary,
   Israel his dominion.

³The sea looked and fled,

the Jordan turned back;
⁴the mountains skipped like rams,
   the hills like lambs.

⁵Why was it, O sea, that you fled,
   O Jordan, that you turned back,
⁶you mountains, that you skipped like rams,
   you hills, like lambs?

⁷Tremble, O earth, at the presence of the LORD,
   at the presence of the God of Jacob,
⁸who turned the rock into a pool
   the hard rock into springs of water.

This is one of the shorter psalms (the shortest is Psalm 117 and the longest 119), but it is rich and profound in its images. The psalm looks back to the exodus and the entry into the Promised Land under Joshua's leadership. We recognize this time reference from the first two verses. While even here there is imagery to note (Judah as God's sanctuary), pay special attention to the next few verses.

The psalmist is reflecting poetically on the parting of the Red Sea (Ex 14—15) and the stopping of the waters of the Jordan (Josh 3). Readers will recognize the imagery found here as *personification*. Personification, by way of reminder, is attributing human characteristics to something nonhuman. A sea doesn't have eyes to see with or legs to flee with. The Jordan River can't turn back like a human. These are images. God is pictured as warring against the sea and the river, and they are so afraid that they attempt to escape (compare with Ps 77:16-20).

The sixth verse continues the imagery. Here is imagery which is even harder for us to understand. How can mountains and hills skip? And what does it mean anyway? The very impact of this verse depends on our inability to interpret it literally. To the ancient Israelite nothing was considered more firm, established and stable than a mountain. But here they are skipping!

The image is relatively common in the Psalms. Its meaning is clearer in other occurrences. Compare this, for instance, with Psalm 29. It pictures God as a great and powerful storm cloud (imagery). His voice stands for thunder (another image). It is God's powerful voice, his presence, which causes the mountains to skip.

From the comparison with Psalm 29, we arrive at a better understanding of the imagery found in Psalm 114:6. Verse 4 is an image of the crossing of the Red Sea and verse 5 of the crossing of the Jordan. Verse 6, therefore, is an image of God's conquest of Canaan for Joshua. The image of the mountains skipping is the image of the powerful presence of God (v. 7) as he brought judgment and war on the Canaanites.

The images in these two psalms show how imagery evokes pictures in our minds.

Types of Images

Simile. Imagery accomplishes these word pictures by means of a comparison. In order to teach us some truth, the psalmist compares it to something else. Occasionally, the comparison is made explicit and is, therefore, a *simile*. A simile, you will recall, is a comparison which is made explicit by the presence of the word *like* or *as*. Here are some examples of similes from the Psalms:

As the deer pants for streams of water,
    so my soul pants for you, O God. (42:1)

This simile compares a thirsty deer looking for water with the psalmist searching for satisfaction in God. The comparison is explicit because of the presence of the word *as*.

O LORD my God, I take refuge in you;
    save and deliver me from all who pursue me,
or they will tear me like a lion
    and rip me to pieces with no one to rescue me. (7:1-2)

This simile is a frequent image in the Scriptures. The enemy is likened to a rending lion. Both are powerful and cruel.

In Psalm 37, a psalm of trust, the enemy is not compared to a beast of prey but rather to grass which will soon be cut down:

Do not fret because of evil men
   or be envious of those who do wrong;
for *like* the grass they will soon wither
   like green plants they will soon die away. (vv. 1-2)
Metaphor. A metaphor, on the other hand, is a comparison
which is implicit. That is, it is a comparison without the mention
of *like* or *as.* Psalm 23 begins:
   The LORD *is* my shepherd, I shall not be in want.
If this were a simile, it would read "The Lord is *like* a shepherd."
A metaphor communicates a more vivid image than a simile
because it is implicit and draws the comparison more closely.

How an Image Works

Now that we understand how to recognize an image in a psalm,
the next step is to examine more closely how the comparison
works. In brief, an image compares two things which are similar
in some ways but dissimilar in other ways. The dissimilarity is
what surprises us and causes us to take notice. Then we search
for the similarity. Examples will make this clear.
   Sons are a heritage from the LORD,
      children a reward from him.
   Like arrows in the hands of a warrior
      are sons born in one's youth.
   Blessed is the man whose quiver is full of them.
   They will not be put to shame when they contend
      with their enemies in the gate. (127:3-5)
This passage is based on a simile. Sons are *like* arrows in the
hands of a warrior. To understand the image we have to ask
ourselves in what way sons are like arrows. To do that we also
need to ask ways in which sons are different from arrows.
   We begin with the obvious. The psalmist does not compare
his sons' physical appearance to the arrows. There is not a
literal, physical correspondence between sons and arrows. But
how are they like each other? How does the comparison with
arrows illuminate the psalmist's contention that sons are a
blessing to their father?
   These arrows belong to a warrior. They are the weapons

which aid him in a battle. Sons are similar in that they are a source of strength to the father as he seeks to make his way in the world. They will support him.

> O LORD, I call to you; come quickly to me.
> Hear my voice when I call to you.
> May my prayer be set before you like incense;
> may the lifting up of my hands be like the evening
> sacrifice. (141:1-2)

Two similes are found at the beginning of Psalm 141. Here we will concentrate on the first. The psalmist's prayer is compared to the incense which is offered up to God in worship. What are the similarities and what are the differences?

The differences are obvious. The similarities take a little more thought, but may be identified in at least two areas: (1) They are both offered up to God, even as the smoke of incense was thought to rise to God; and (2) they are both holy and precious to God (see the description of the incense in Ex 30:34-38).

Why Images?

Why are there so many metaphors and similes in the Psalms? What do they add to the message of the Psalms?

First of all, it must be admitted that images are not as precise as literal language. They don't point to the truth of the psalm as directly as a literal statement does. In other words, they do not reduce easily to statements of fact.

Remember that precision is different from accuracy. A metaphor may be less precise than a literal sentence and still be without error. To say "the enemy is ruthless and cruel" is more precise than to say "the enemy is a lion," but both are accurate.

But why not be precise all the time? Why bother with images? When using images, whatever is lost in precision is gained in vividness of expression. Further, the images, as in poetry in general, speak to us more fully than regular literal language.[1] They stir our emotions, attract our attention and also stimulate our imaginations as well as help us discover some new truth about the objects compared.

We can illustrate all of these points with another example. At the end of Psalm 78 we find the following simile:
Then the Lord awoke as from sleep,
   as a man wakes from the stupor of wine.
He beat back his enemies;
   he put them to everlasting shame. (vv. 65-66)
This image gets our attention immediately! The comparison is between the Lord and a man arising after a deep sleep. What is more, almost shockingly, the man's sleep is deep as the result of consuming too much wine. Now that the image has grabbed our attention, what do we discover from it?

The psalm as a whole concerns the rebellious history of Israel particularly in the wilderness. As a result of their rebelliousness, God "gave his people over to the sword" (v. 62). In other words, he wasn't present with them; he was absent from them.

The last few verses (vv. 65-72) describe how God made his presence dwell with Israel again during David's time. It was as if God were sleeping and now had awakened to help his people. The picture is vivid and striking and communicates its point well and in a way that can't fully be paraphrased in literal language. This is because images speak not only to our minds but to our hearts and wills as well.

Turning briefly to a more traditional image, consider again the beginning of Psalm 23.
The LORD is my shepherd; I shall not be in want. (v. 1)
A partial paraphrase of the image would be that God takes care of us because he loves us and guides us in life. Why not say it that way? It is more precise after all. Indeed the Bible in other places does say it in a straightforward manner, but the image of the shepherd speaks to our hearts more directly.

We know how a shepherd lives with his sheep, tends to their every need, keeps them from getting lost and protects them from wild beasts. All of these characteristics and more come to mind when God is called a shepherd. It would take a page of prose to communicate what the psalmist has stated in a clause, and it would do so with less impact.

Biblical Imagery and the Modern Reader

God did not speak to his people in a cultural vacuum. He spoke in terms that they understood. Since the Psalms originated in an ancient, oriental society, the imagery arises from that culture.

Thus, much of the imagery is foreign to modern, Western experience. Very few people who were born and bred in London or New York City have had firsthand experience as shepherds. Accordingly, they do not have the same immediate understanding of the shepherd imagery of Psalm 23 as an ancient Israelite would have had. A twentieth-century Christian living near sheep farms in Wisconsin or Yorkshire would have a clearer understanding of what the psalm is communicating, but even here there are differences between modern and ancient, Western and oriental shepherds.

Further, for those who have never seen the grand and majestic mountains of Lebanon, the impact of Psalm 29:6 is lessened:

He [the Lord] made Lebanon skip like a calf,
Sirion like a young wild ox.

Our understanding of the meaning of an ancient biblical image comes about through, in the first place, imagining ourselves to be hearing the psalm for the first time when it was originally composed. We need to learn through reading, for instance, what were the customs of shepherds in the ancient Near East. In our study, we will discover that the shepherd image was a common one for rulers, so that Psalm 23 has something to contribute to the biblical theme of God as king.

Thus, it is important to first of all realize that the imagery of the Psalter is foreign to us. Second, we must ask how the first readers of the psalm would have understood the imagery. We may discover the original meaning of the imagery by studying commentaries and books about Old Testament background.

Mythological Allusions in the Psalms

Before leaving the subject of imagery, we must notice one specific type of image. Interestingly enough, this is imagery based

on the religions of Israel's neighbors.
> But you, O God, are my king from of old;
>   you bring salvation upon the earth.
> It was you who split open the sea by your power;
>   you broke the heads of the monster in the waters.
> It was you who crushed the heads of Leviathan
>   and gave him as food to the creatures of the desert.
>   (74:12-14)

Here God is pictured as the one who killed the great sea monster whose name is Leviathan. It is further mentioned that he destroyed the many-headed monster by a blow to the head.

What is interesting about this image is that both the Canaanites and the Babylonians believed that *their* main god destroyed the sea monster. The Canaanites had stories about Baal destroying a god named Sea (Yamm) by crushing his head,[2] and the Babylonians believed that their chief god Marduk killed a goddess named Sea (Tiamat).

What is the psalm saying then? Is it agreeing with the pagan religions of their neighbors? Far from it! God's destruction of Leviathan in Psalm 74 is an image of his power. Further, there is a message to the pagan nations here and to those Israelites tempted to worship foreign gods. That message implicitly stated is: "Your gods are nothing; our God is everything. You think your gods showed their power by defeating the forces of chaos (for this is what the sea stood for). You are wrong. It was Yahweh the God of the Israelites, our God."

Such allusions are not uncommon in the Psalter and elsewhere. They are not borrowings from the surrounding religions, but rather a form of missions, particularly to the Israelites who had gone over to their neighbors' religion.

One more example will make this clear. Psalm 48 begins:
> Great is the LORD,
>   and most worthy of praise,
> in the city of our God,
>   his holy mountain.
> It is beautiful in its loftiness,
>   the joy of the whole earth.

Like the utmost heights of Zaphon is Mount Zion. (vv. 1-2)
This psalm is well known, but you may not recognize the translation of the last colon. Older translations like the King James
translate it *is mount Zion, on the sides of the north.*

For various reasons most translators and interpreters have
come to see that the King James Version cannot be right here
and that there is a reference to the mountain Zaphon. Hence
the translation above (quoted from the New International Version).

Mount Zion then is compared to a place called Zaphon (notice this is a simile). What is Zaphon? Here background becomes important. We know from other ancient Near Eastern
texts that Zaphon is the mountain where the god Baal was
thought to dwell. It was an imposing mountain, fit to be the
dwelling place of such a powerful god.

Psalm 48 compares Zion, the mountain on which the temple
was built, with Zaphon. The purpose of this comparison was to
claim for Zion what was claimed for Zaphon by Baal worshipers (and there were plenty of these in Israel during the Old
Testament period). God dwelt on Zion, not on Zaphon. Yahweh, the God of Israel, was the true and only God. Baal was
nothing.

These mythological allusions serve to show that Yahweh, the
God of the Old Testament, is vastly superior to the manmade
deities of Israel's neighbors. In this way certain psalms function
the way 1 Kings 18 does, the story of Elijah on Mount Carmel.
In this dramatic story, Elijah takes on 450 prophets of Baal and
400 prophets of Asherah. Elijah claims that Yahweh, not Baal,
will light the fire of the sacrificial altar on Mount Carmel.

To understand the full force of the story, we must realize that
God is fighting on Baal's supposed ground. The one who
throws fire down from heaven to light the fire wins. Baal is
supposed to be a specialist in this since the Canaanites believed
that he was a rain god, the god of lightning in other words.

Of course, Elijah, although outnumbered and also making
things difficult for himself by pouring water on the wood,
wins—since Baal is nonexistent, an idol constructed by the

minds of sinful people. God has shown that he is the true provider of the rains. This is an important issue in the broader context since the land was experiencing a life-threatening drought at the time.

Most readers of the book of Psalms will miss this aspect of a psalm's message because few people today know much about Canaanite, Egyptian or Babylonian religion. Nonetheless, we will miss an important part of a psalm's message if we don't recognize an allusion to a pagan religion.

Commentaries are the best means of learning about the background of the Psalms. However, commentaries should always be read with a critical mind. After all, they differ with one another; they can't all be right. However, they are usually written by scholars who specialize in the Old Testament and who know Near Eastern languages and literature. Commentators will frequently inform readers about a mythological allusion.

I have listed a number of commentaries on the Psalms at the end of the book, with evaluations of their strong and weak points.

Metaphor and the Incomprehensibility of God

I began this chapter by listing a few of the many images used to describe God in the Psalms. Why are there so many? The answer may lie in God's own nature.

Briefly, the answer is this: images, particularly metaphors, help to communicate the fact that God is so great and powerful and mighty that he can't be exhaustively described. Metaphor, we have seen, may be accurate, but is less precise than literal language. Metaphor preserves the mystery of God's nature and being, while communicating to us about him and his love for us.

Suggestions for Psalm Study

26. Be aware that an image is likely to exist when it is impossible or absurd to interpret a word, sentence or section literally.

27. While reading a psalm, be sensitive to imagery. Imagery compares one thing to another. If the comparison is explicit

(like or *as)*, then the image is a simile. If the comparison is implicit, then the image is a metaphor.

28. When interpreting an image, identify the comparison which is being made.

29. Think seriously about the comparison. In what ways are the two things alike and in what ways are they different?

30. Be aware that the imagery of the Psalter comes from the culture of ancient Israel and not the modern West.

31. Images may come from non-Israelite religions. But when they do, they are adapted for a very specific purpose. The use of such images is polemical. That is, they communicated to pagans and probably more directly to apostate Israelites that they were worshiping the wrong god. The power was with Israel's God.

32. Have some good commentaries handy. Refer to them *after* having thought about the meaning of the psalm.

Exercises

1. Identify the similes in Psalms 52 and 83.

2. Identify the metaphors in Psalms 80 and 129.

3. Read Psalm 124. One major image in this psalm is water. In the first part of the psalm, the psalmist's troubles are likened to overwhelming waters (vv. 4-5). Meditate on this metaphor by determining in what way the overwhelming water illuminates the depths of the psalmist's suffering.

4. Search through Psalms 30—35. List all the images of God that you find. Consider how great, mighty and loving your God is in the light of these images.

Further Reading

Caird, G. B. *The Language and Imagery of the Bible*. Philadelphia: Westminster Press, 1980.

Hawkes, T. *Metaphor*. Critical Inquiry 25. London: Methuen, 1972.

Keel, O. *The Symbolism of the Biblical World*. New York: Seabury, 1978.

*Ricoeur, P. *The Rule of Metaphor*. trans. by R. Czerny. Toronto: University of Toronto Press, 1977.

Part III
A Melody
of Psalms

9
Psalm 98: Let
Earth Praise
Our Warrior

We have covered much ground since the first chapter. We have looked closely at the Psalms by asking how elements of poetry such as parallelism and metaphor communicate to us. We have also studied whole psalms and observed that they fall into about seven different genres. We even discussed how the Psalms relate to the rest of the Bible and also to our lives.

Along the way we have used examples of each point made. In addition, through the exercises at the end of the chapters, we have been applying the principles of interpretation taught in this book.

To bring matters to a close, however, we will examine three psalms in more detail. Even by restricting ourselves to three examples, we will not have space to study them exhaustively. Only occasionally will we be able to closely describe the parallelism. Our analysis, however, will always be based on this kind of close reading. I hope that the following comments will stimulate your further meditation on these psalms and on other similar psalms.

In this chapter we will study Psalm 98, a hymn of praise to

avior, King, judge and warrior. In chapter ten we will
a lament with which our hearts resonate when we are
treme distress, Psalm 69. Then in chapter eleven we will
d with a thanksgiving psalm, Psalm 30.

To see that Psalm 98 is a hymn all we have to do is read it:

Stanza 1
A Sing to the LORD a new song,
B   for he has done wonderful acts;
C his right hand and his holy arm have saved them.
          (v. 1)
D The LORD has made his salvation known—
E   in the presence of the nations—
F he has revealed his righteousness. (v. 2)
G He remembered his covenant love and his faithfulness
                to the house of Israel;
H all the ends of the earth have seen the salvation of our
          God. (v 3)

Stanza 2
Shout for joy to the LORD, all the earth.
Break forth and sing for joy and sing praise. (v. 4)
Sing praise to the LORD with a lyre,
with a lyre and the sound of playing, (v. 5)
with a trumpet and the sound of the horn,
shout for joy before the King, Yahweh. (v. 6)

Stanza 3
Let the sea storm and all its fullness,
     the world and all who dwell therein. (v. 7)
Let the rivers clap (their) hands,
     Let the mountains together sing for joy before the LORD,
          (v. 8)
for he is coming to judge the earth,
     he will judge the world with righteousness
     and the peoples with equity. (v. 9, translation mine
               throughout psalm)

This song bursts at the seams as it praises God! The mood is unmistakable. As a hymn, it has two characteristic parts: call to worship and the reasons for the praise (introduced by the tell-tale *for* in v. 1).

But now that we have recognized the genre of Psalm 98, we want to look more closely at its structure and message. Each hymn has its own unique structure as well as sharing the general structure of a hymn. As we look closely we notice quickly that the psalm has three parts. These three parts are separated by their different reasons for praise, their time references and the expanding circle of praise.

Stanza 1

The first stanza has three poetic lines. The first line has three poetic phrases *(A-C)*. In the first phrase the psalmist opens with a call to Israel to praise the Lord. The next two phrases give the reason behind the command to worship. Specifically, the psalmist praises God for the salvation with which God has delivered Israel in the past.

The deliverance is not named in the psalm, but that's not surprising since earlier we learned that psalms do not name specific historical events. Psalm 98 accordingly was used to praise God for the many times he saved Israel in the past. As the Old Testament faithful read the first stanza of Psalm 98, they would think of the exodus, the wars won under Joshua, the times God delivered Israel from foreign oppressors during the period of the Judges, the deliverance from the Philistines under David, and so on down to the time when God brought the remnant safely back from Babylon.

Why has God delivered Israel? Verse 3 cites God's covenant love *(ḥesed)* and his faithfulness. The Israelites were God's people. They were no better than any other nation (Deut 7:7-11), but God loved them nonetheless and determined to bless the nations through Israel (Gen 12:3). Our psalm concurs by proclaiming that God's deliverance was displayed before the whole world.

The universal witness to God's deliverance of Israel is emphasized in both the second and third lines of stanza 1. The second line *(D, E, F)* is a pivot pattern where the middle phrase *(E)* is read with both the first *(D)* and the third *(F)* phrases. In this way, the middle phrase "in the presence of the nations" is underlined and the universal witness of God's acts is revealed. But, nonetheless, as far as the first stanza is concerned only Israel praises the Lord. The other nations have merely "seen" the acts of God. This point is also the message of the third line of the stanza *(G, H)*. Here we observe a bicolon in which the second phrase *(H)* is the result of what is described in the first *(G)*. As God reveals his love to Israel, the nations see the salvation of God.

Stanza 2

The praise gets louder in the next three verses which make up the second stanza. Now, not just Israel, but *the whole earth* is called upon to shout to the Lord with joy.

This is a noisy stanza. The stanza piles praise upon praise to God. All kinds of music are mentioned from singing to harp, to trumpets, to rams' horn—all are to join in praising God.

We must be careful, though, to see the object of praise through the happy din. At the very end of the stanza we are told that all our praise is to be directed toward God, *our King!*

Israel had a human king ever since the time of Saul. Faithful Israelites, however, knew that this human king, even if he was as blessed as David, was only a pale reflection of the true King, Yahweh.

So, we have moved from a call to Israel to praise God as Savior in the past to a call to the whole earth to praise God as its present King. Where do we go from here?

Stanza 3

It's hard to believe, but the praise gets even louder! Not only do Israel and the whole earth praise God, but *the entire universe* praises him. Further, the call to praise goes beyond people to the whole of creation. Everyone and everything will praise God!

Even nature, specifically the rivers and mountains, praises

God. This is appropriate because, after all, God created nature as well as people (Ps 95:3-5).

Of course, the reference to the rivers clapping their hands is a poetic figure of speech. It is personification. An inanimate object is given the powers and abilities of a person. We will not (and cannot) interpret these verses literally. Nevertheless, it is especially appropriate that nature joins the circle of praise in the third stanza. The object of worship in the third stanza is, of course, God again, but this time in his role as a judge, the coming judge.

According to Romans the creation yearns for the coming judgment:

I consider that our present sufferings are not worth comparing with the glory that will be revealed in us. The creation waits in eager expectation for the sons of God to be revealed. For the creation was subjected to frustration, not by its own choice, but by the will of the one who subjected it, in hope that the creation itself will be liberated from its bondage to decay and brought into the glorious freedom of the children of God.

We know that the whole creation has been groaning as in the pains of childbirth right up to the present time. Not only so, but we ourselves, who have the firstfruits of the Spirit, groan inwardly as we wait eagerly for our adoption as sons, the redemption of our bodies. For in this hope we were saved. But hope that is seen is no hope at all. Who hopes for what he already has? But if we hope for what we do not yet have, we wait for it patiently.

In the same way, the Spirit helps us in our weakness. We do not know what we ought to pray, but the Spirit himself intercedes for us with groans that words cannot express. And he who searches our hearts knows the mind of the Spirit, because the Spirit intercedes for the saints in accordance with God's will. (Rom 8:18-27)

This New Testament text explains that when Adam and Eve sinned and fell from the grace of God (Gen 3), all creation fell under covenant curse. How horrible it is to live in a fallen world—a world subjected to vanity, without God—is the theme of an entire Old Testament book, the book of Ecclesiastes. In any case, we and the whole creation look to the future judgment of God for freedom from the curse.

Thus, we have seen that Psalm 98 is a hymn to God in three movements. These three movements may be summarized in the following way:

1. Israel is to praise God for saving them in the past (vv. 1-3).

2. All the earth is to praise God for being King in the present (vv. 4-6).

3. The entire universe is to praise God for coming to judge in the future (vv. 7-9).

God is praised as savior, king and judge! What is amazing is that these three attributes of God are all connected with one major theme in the Old and New Testaments, the picture of God as a warrior who commits himself to protect his faithful people.

Turn back to Exodus 15 and read the Song of Moses. This song was sung in celebration of the great victory over Egypt which God won for Israel at the Red Sea. It is a song of praise very similar to Psalm 98, but it is deeply embedded in a specific historical deliverance. Notice the language of Exodus 15:3:

The LORD is a warrior;
the LORD is his name.

Exodus 15 sings a song of praise to God as Divine Warrior. God and his heavenly army come to fight for Israel against the Egyptian army. God as a warrior is a theme which reverberates through the whole Old Testament. God battles for Israel again at the walls of Jericho (Josh 6), outside of Jerusalem as David defeats the Philistines (2 Sam 5:17-25), and against Moab as Jehoshaphat goes to war (2 Chron 20).

In Psalm 98 God shows himself to be a warrior as he saves his people from their enemies by the power of "his right hand and his holy arm" (98:1). He shows himself to be a warrior as he judges the wicked (stanza 3). And when God wins the victory, he is once again affirmed as King (stanza 2 and Ex 15:18).[1]

After a close look at Psalm 98 it is clear that this song was used throughout the period of the Old Testament to celebrate the victories which God won for Israel. Indeed, it is likely that it was sung especially at the time when the army returned from battle and as faithful Israel rightly attributed the victory to God, the Divine Warrior.

But what does that have to do with us? We don't fight battles against Canaanites. As a matter of fact, we're told to put away the sword (Mt 26:52-56) and show love toward our enemies.

This is true, but we must not forget that we are engaged in a war much more dangerous than the wars which Joshua fought. That war is not against flesh and blood but "against the rulers, against the authorities, against the powers of this dark world and against the spiritual forces of evil in the heavenly realms" (Eph 6:12). In this battle we need to call on the power of God. Ephesians 6 remarkably describes our struggles in military or Divine Warrior language: "put on the full armor of God." Psalm 98 helps us to remember the warfare we are engaged in and to call on God to deliver us.[2]

As we meditate upon Psalm 98 from a New Testament perspective, we note how appropriately the psalm fits into our own lives and our relationship with Jesus Christ:

1. Stanza 1: Praise Jesus who has saved us in the past.
2. Stanza 2: Praise Jesus who is our king in the present.
3. Stanza 3: Praise Jesus who is coming as judge in the future.

Finally, in connection with Jesus Christ as future judge we think of the picture of the Second Coming painted in Revelation, a picture of Jesus as a warrior who will do away with evil once and for all.

I saw heaven standing open and there before me was a white horse, whose rider is called Faithful and True. With justice he judges and makes war. His eyes are like blazing fire, and on his head are many crowns. . . . The armies of heaven were following him. . . . Out of his mouth comes a sharp sword with which to strike down the nations. (Rev 19:11-21)

10
Psalm 69:
Lord, I Suffer
for Your Sake

The **lives of** obedient Christians are always fulfilling, but never easy. As Christians, we have something which the world lacks—Christ who brings meaning to our lives. Nonetheless, as long as we are in the world we will confront hostility, frustration, fear and danger.

The laments speak to us when we are distressed and depressed, and Psalm 69 is a frank and powerful example of a personal lament. As we will see, David's lament arises because he is suffering undeservedly for his obedience to God.

As we study this psalm, ask yourself if you can identify with the psalmist. Most of us can easily see ourselves in the description which the psalmist draws of his trouble.

Much of Psalm 69 will sound familiar to you from the New Testament. This psalm is the second most quoted psalm in the New Testament. It is second only to Psalm 22, another individual lament.

The psalm is a long one, too long to quote here in full. So it's a good idea to open a Bible and read the psalm before going on.

There is no doubt that Psalm 69 is a lament. The mood is one of tearful complaint to God. Obviously, the psalmist is shaken by his circumstances, and he turns to God for help.

Besides the mood, however, the structure leads us to recognize Psalm 69 as a lament. Laments were described in chapter one as composed of seven different parts, and Psalm 69 contains all seven: invocation, plea for help, complaints, confession, imprecation, expression of confidence, and hymn.

The psalm is unique, though, among personal laments for the way these seven parts are distributed. For instance, the complaint is divided into three parts and spreads through the whole psalm. This obviously emphasizes the complaint of the psalmist and shows that he urgently and tearfully appeals to God for help. He can't get away from his complaints.

Instead of commenting on the psalm verse by verse, I will describe each of the seven elements of the psalm. Before beginning this, however, a couple of comments on the psalm's title are in order.

Title
We get three bits of information about the psalm from the title. The first is that the psalm is "for the chief musician." While the titles, this one included, are difficult to translate and fully understand, this note leads us to believe that the psalm was composed and used with music. It also connects the psalm with the formal worship of Israel, since the chief musician was probably a person like Asaph who was in charge of music for the worship of God (1 Chron 16:4-6).

The second piece of information we get is truly mysterious, "to the lilies." The best guess as to the meaning of this phrase is that "lilies" is the tune to which the psalm was sung. Many translations, including The New International Version, go so far as to translate it *To the [tune of] "Lilies."*

The last part of the title informs us that David composed it. This is accepted by Paul in Romans 11:9-10, who introduces a quote from our psalm with the comment that it was composed by David.

The psalm lacks a historical title. The historical titles connect psalms with a particular event in the life of David (see chapter five). Many commentators make the error of expending the bulk of their energies recovering the historical setting of the psalm from hints within the text. However, this psalm, like all psalms, is purposefully nonspecific. As a result, the psalm may be used on many different occasions, even in our lives, though we live almost three thousand years after the psalm was composed.

Invocation and Initial Plea to God for Help (v. 1)

The psalm begins with an invocation. The psalmist pleads with God to save him from his distress. He simply cries out, "Save me, O God!" He can't hold back from God his urgent cry.

We can learn about prayer from the psalmist. As we study the laments, we are continually reminded of the frank way in which the psalmist speaks to God. He tells God how he is feeling and what he is thinking in no uncertain terms. Some Christians tend to pray to God as if we can hide from him what's really going on in our minds. We should be honest with God if we're impatient with him or angry with him or disappointed in him. We certainly won't fool him if we bottle it up inside of ourselves.

Complaints (vv. 1-4, 7-12, 19-21)

In the complaint sections we learn why the psalmist is lamenting, and we continue to see him being honest with God. There are three separate complaint sections, and in each he uses powerful images to communicate his situation to God.

The psalmist paints a vivid picture in the first complaint section—the end of verse 1 through verse 4. He describes his condition metaphorically as that of a person who is caught in the midst of a river and is slowly sinking into the muddy bottom while the raging waters are threatening to engulf him. Notice the poetic progression in verse 2:

I have come into the deep waters;
    the floods engulf me.

What a graphic picture of being overwhelmed with troubles! We understand what the psalmist is talking about here. We have

all felt overwhelmed by guilt or persecution or heavy respon-
sibilities at one time or another.

Nonetheless, we still must put ourselves in the place of the
ancient Israelite poet to gain a full appreciation of this image.
Water, especially churned-up water, was a pointed image of
chaos and even death in the ancient Near East. This is clear
throughout the Old Testament. The author of Psalm 46 cannot
imagine a worse situation than the mountains falling into the
sea (v. 2). Ultimate horror is communicated by Daniel as he tells
us of his vision of four hybrid creatures coming out of a "churn-
ing" sea (Dan 7:2-14).

In verse 4 we begin to hear what is bothering David. He is
being persecuted. His enemies are accusing him of theft! The
historical books record no such accusation against David, perhaps because the books of Samuel and Chronicles are highly
selective. Or it may be that the reference to stealing is metaphorical. The verse would then mean that the psalmist is being
punished for things which he did not do.

The reason for the psalmist's lament, though, goes far
beyond the number of his enemies or their false accusation.
His tears flow because he feels abandoned by God. He has
been crying to God, but he gets no answer! He has been calling
to God so much, in fact, that his throat is dry and his eyes are
full of tears. "Where are you, God?"

In the second complaint section (vv. 7-12) it becomes clear
that the psalmist suffers because of his devotion to God: "I
endure scorn for your sake" (v. 7). In verse 9 he cries out, "Zeal
for your house consumes me." These words sound very familiar, for Jesus takes them on his lips as he cleanses the temple
(Jn 2:17).

David likely has the tabernacle in mind, since the temple
would not be built until Solomon's reign. However, the verses
may have reference to David's zeal to prepare for the building
of the temple, a task which, according to 1 Chronicles 22, he
took very seriously.

But, once again, the psalm is not historically specific, so that
everyone who endures scorn for the cause of God may identify

with the psalmist. Indeed, we may lift up our voices with the psalmist.

By the time we come to the third complaint section (vv. 19-21), the psalmist is utterly exhausted: "Scorn has broken my heart" (v. 20). His enemies surrounded him, so he looked to his friends for support. Instead of help, he laments that they "put gall in my food and gave me vinegar for my thirst" (v. 21).

Once again, these words sound familiar to us from the life of Jesus. In the psalm, the reference is metaphoric. He is implicitly likening his need for encouragement to the need of a hungry man for food and a thirsty man for drink. Those he turns to for help are like those who would give him inedible food and a drink which would only increase his thirst.

Confession of Sin (vv. 5-6)

In the first complaint the psalmist denies the wrongdoing of which he is accused (v. 4). Nonetheless, he does recognize that he is not completely innocent:

You know my folly, O God;
   my guilt is not hidden from you. (v. 5)

Such a confession of sin is not uncommon in the laments (compare 51:3-6). The psalmist frequently admits his sin to God before turning to him for help.

Some Christians neglect this aspect of prayer to their detriment. True, we are forgiven in Christ, but this does not give us a license to sin (Rom 6:1-7)! The sad truth is that we do continue to sin. Thus, we must constantly come before our forgiving Lord in repentance if we expect to grow in our faith. We can learn how to do this by meditating on the laments of the Psalms.

The confession section of Psalm 69 includes an appeal to God that:

those who hope in you not be disgraced because of me,
   O Lord, the LORD Almighty;
may those who seek you not be put to shame because of me,
   O God of Israel. (v. 6)

David asks that the reputation of other faithful Israelites not be tainted because of his sin. Once again we learn from the Psalms. It is often true that our sins damage the reputation and the ministry of other Christians.

Further Pleas for Help (vv. 13-18)
The logical thing to do after confessing sins to the Lord and bringing our troubles before him is to ask him to help us in the midst of our difficulties. This is precisely what the psalmist does. His plea for help is found in verses 13-18.

David turns to the Lord in prayer and earnestly asks for God's "sure salvation" (v. 13). He appeals to God's grace and his love as the basis of his expectation that God will deliver him (vv. 13, 16).

In verses 13 and 14 he picks up the metaphoric language with which he complained before the Lord:
Rescue me from the mire,
    do not let me sink;
deliver me from those who hate me,
    from the deep waters. (v. 14)

Imprecation (vv. 22-28)
The psalmist, however, does not stop with his request for his own salvation. He desires the destruction of his enemies (vv. 22-28), and this is often hard for us to understand:
Pour out your wrath on them;
    let your fierce anger overtake them. . . .
May they be blotted out of the book of life
    and not be listed with the righteous. (vv. 24, 28)
Curse or imprecation upon enemies is frequently found in the Psalms. How are we to understand these curses? They seem so wrong to us who are instructed to love our enemies (Mt 5:43-48). We are called to put away the sword (Mt 26:52) and to share the gospel in love with those who persecute us.

Two errors must be avoided. On the one hand, some Christians argue that we are not to pray these same prayers because they are not God's words, but rather the psalmist's very human expression of hate.[1] The psalmist falls short of the Christian ideal because he lived before the time of Christ. But if this is true, it reflects on the whole book of Psalms and raises the question, How can we treat any part of the psalms as canonical?

On the other hand, other Christians feel that we can pray these psalms just as the psalmist did. Those who persecute us, or at least those who commit gross sins against the church and humanity (Hitler, Khomeni, Amin, the leadership of North Korea are examples I have heard) are appropriately cursed by the church. However, this does not take into account the radical love to which Jesus calls us.

But we are left with a problem. How can we say it was all right for the psalmist, but wrong for us, to pray these prayers against personal enemies?

Only a tentative answer can be given here. As we study the Scriptures from Genesis to Revelation, we see that God radically changes our relationship with people outside the community of God. In the Old Testament the Israelites were to be holy and separate. The nations were to flow to them. In addition, God illustrated his judgment on sin by occasionally ordering his people to take up the sword against Israel's enemies (the Conquest).

In the New Testament, the warfare has gotten more serious. The Christian is not to fight against unbelievers. Indeed, that is sin on the highest order. But we are to pick up the sword "against the spiritual forces of evil in the heavenly realms" (Eph 6:12).

Thus, while it is still hard for us to understand God's ways in the Old Testament, we can see that David appropriately prayed such a prayer, but that we cannot pray the same prayer in the same way. The curses of the Psalms are wrongly used if applied to a person.

However, since our warfare is against Satan and the spiritual forces of evil, we may call down our curses upon them. How can we do that? In a number of ways. Perhaps the most dramatic way we can pray against Satan is to pray for the conversion of unbelievers. Indeed, evangelism is the primary form of Christian Holy War against the powers of darkness. The New

Testament teaches us that those who are not devoted to Christ are slaves of Satan. When such a slave becomes a Christian, he or she dies, that is, the old man dies. The new man is raised with Christ (Col 2:6-23). We should also know that when we pray for Christ to come again, we are praying for the final destruction of Satan and his followers, both human and spiritual.

Hymn of Praise (vv. 30-36)
The last section of this psalm is a hymn of praise (vv. 30-36). Notice the abrupt transition between verses 29 and 30:
> I am in pain and distress;
>> may your salvation, O God, protect me.
> I will praise God's name in song.

What has happened? We can't be sure, but, based on the strong probability that this psalm was used in a formal worship setting, we may imagine that a priest was present who gave a word of assurance after the man or woman who prayed finished the lament. We have already observed, however, that the movement from grief to joy is a common feature of laments.

The psalmist rejoices that his praise will:
> please the LORD more than an ox,
>> more than a bull with its horns and hoofs. (v. 31)

His simple prayer is more precious to God than an expensive sacrifice! That is indeed good news to the poor (v. 32) who couldn't afford to burn an ox.

Psalm 69 is the heartfelt cry of David as he suffers at the hands of evil men and women, particularly as they ridicule him for his devotion to God. The psalm itself, though, is not closely tied to David, so it became the earnest plea of all who suffer undeservedly as they seek to serve God.

Though the psalm is fully understandable in its Old Testament context, the many times which the New Testament quotes it in reference to Jesus' ministry pushes us forward.

This is a psalm which may be sung to Jesus. When we are persecuted because of righteousness, we may lift up our voices to God for help.

It is also a song which is sung by Jesus (see chapter four), when as a suffering Messiah he identified with the laments in the Psalter. As he cleansed the temple, he identified with the psalmist's zeal which led to his persecution. Further, Paul compared the selfless way in which Christ suffered with the suffering of the psalmist, when in Romans 15:3 he quotes Psalm 69:9.

There is one dramatic change in Jesus' use of the psalm which catches our attention, though. We have observed that the psalmist describes the evil way his friends treat him when they put gall in his food and vinegar in his drink. While this was a figurative expression in the psalm, it literally happened to Jesus. As he hung on the cross, they offered him drinks with gall and later vinegar (Mt 27:34, 48).

The dramatic difference is in Christ's reaction. The psalmist passes immediately from the metaphor to a strong curse on his enemies (vv. 22-28). Jesus, on the contrary, had an attitude of forgiveness toward those who crucified him: "Father, forgive them, for they do not know what they are doing" (Lk 23:34).

11
Psalm 30:
Thank You, Lord,
for Healing Me!

We have moved from the height of joy (Ps 98) down to the pits of grief (Ps 69). Now we are going to ascend again from the abyss with Psalm 30. Psalm 30 is a prayer thanking God for answering a previous prayer.

As we have observed, thanksgivings are closely related to hymns. As a matter of fact, the Hebrew word for "thanksgiving" *(tôdāh)* is formed from a verb which means "to praise" *(yādāh).*

Thanksgivings are further related to laments, since the former is seen as an answer to the latter. Walter Brueggemann has helpfully divided the Psalms into three categories.[1] First are psalms of *orientation* (hymns) which praise God for being God. The psalmist's world is in order. The laments are psalms of *disorientation.* The psalmist has lost his way. He experiences fear and grief. Finally, there are psalms of *reorientation,* which experience renewed hope in God. The thanksgivings in general, and Psalm 30 in particular, are in this category.[2]

As we turn to this thanksgiving psalm, we need to realize that we are at the heart of what it means to be a Christian. It surprises us to realize this. We sometimes think that what makes Christians different from non-Christians is that we know that

God exists. Certainly, that's crucial, but Romans 1:21 teaches us
that everyone *knows* God. Strikingly, Paul here tells us that the
real difference between a Christian and a non-Christian is that
the former *gives thanks* to God. Remember the story of Jesus and
the ten men whom he healed from leprosy (Lk 17:11-19). Of
the ten, only one returned to thank him.

With that in mind, read this thanksgiving psalm of David:

A psalm. A song. For the dedication of the temple. Of David.
¹I will exalt you, O LORD,
    for you lifted me out of the depths
    and did not let my enemies gloat over me.
²O LORD my God, I called to you for help
    and you healed me.
³O LORD, you brought me up from the grave;
    you spared me from going down into the pit.
⁴Sing to the LORD, you saints of his;
    praise his holy name.
⁵For his anger lasts only a moment,
    but his favor lasts a lifetime;
weeping may remain for a night,
    but rejoicing comes in the morning.
⁶When I felt secure, I said,
    "I will never be shaken."
⁷O LORD, when you favored me,
    you made my mountain stand firm;
but when you hid your face,
    I was dismayed.
⁸To you, O LORD, I called;
    to the Lord I cried for mercy:
⁹"What gain is there in my destruction,
    in my going down into the pit?
Will the dust praise you?
    Will it proclaim your faithfulness?
¹⁰Hear, O LORD, and be merciful to me;
    O LORD, be my help."
¹¹You turned my wailing into dancing;

you removed my sackcloth and clothed me with joy,
[12]that my heart may sing to you and not be silent.
O LORD my God, I will give you thanks forever.

Title

The title first informs us of this psalm's genre. Unfortunately, we cannot be sure what the difference was between a "psalm" and a "song." The Hebrew word "psalm" *(mizmôr)* is a noun based on a verb "to sing" *(zāmar)*. Both words indicate a musical setting for the psalm.

The difficulty continues with what appears to be a functional title, though it might be interpreted as a title telling how the psalm was used: "for the dedication of the temple." It is not immediately obvious how this title relates to the psalm's content, so we will not force our interpretation of the psalm to artificially conform with it (see chapter two).

David is cited as the author. Once again, there is no reason to doubt that David wrote it, but we will not allow our historical curiosity to distract us into a fruitless debate concerning the event in David's life which motivated the composition of Psalm 30.

The Psalm

Since thanksgivings are so similar to hymns, it is not surprising that Psalm 30 begins with a strong statement of praise. The psalmist makes clear his intention from the very start when he says, "I will exalt you, O Lord."

His declaration of praise leads him to cite reasons. He first states it figuratively, though English translations usually don't make the metaphor obvious. David praises God because God lifted him out of the depths. The verb *(dālāh)* elsewhere literally means to lift a bucket up from a well. The verb evokes an image in our minds. The psalmist had fallen into a well and the Lord helped him up.

This saving act of God silenced the psalmist's enemies (v. 1). The "enemies" play as prominent a role in the thanksgivings as in the laments. Here they rejoice over the psalmist's suffering. Verses 2 and 3 make clear how God saved the psalmist. He had been ill, so ill that he almost died. God had healed him from his physical distress.

To truly understand Psalm 30 we must apply it to our own lives. Do we rejoice when God heals us from sickness and disease? Or do we pray for his help and then conveniently forget him when he answers?

The psalmist doesn't forget God's goodness. He not only thanks God, but he directs the people of God to praise him. The "sharing times" that occur in modern church services and fellowship groups are too often an excuse to praise ourselves. The psalmist is a model for "sharing" as he directs the attention of the congregation away from himself and toward God.

Further, the psalmist asks God's saints to praise him. When we hear the word *saints,* we tend to think of dead believers. The word here translated "saints" *(ḥasidim)* is related to a Hebrew word with which we have already become acquainted *(ḥesed),* which I have suggested translates as "covenant lovingkindness." Thus, these saints are those who are in a covenant relationship, a personal relationship, with God.

As a result of his personal experience of God's grace, David expresses a general truth about God in verse 5. It is memorable, at least in part, because of its antithetical structure (see chapter seven). Notice how he contrasts God's anger and his favor. Remember too that the psalmist has recently felt God's curse and now enjoys his blessing:

For his anger lasts only a moment,
    but his favor lasts a lifetime;
weeping may remain for a night,
    but rejoicing comes in the morning. (v. 5)

As part of his testimony to God, the psalmist recounts the situation which led to his need. He's not bashful to share his sin. His sin is pride or self-confidence according to verses 6 and 7. He had put his strength in his own power when he said "I will never be shaken." Then God "hid his face." After becoming ill, the psalmist knew that it was God who was the cause of both his prosperity and his health.

He became ill, threatened with death. He quotes his complaint to God in verse 9. As Christians we have a hard time relating to the psalmist's line of argument. He seems to barter with God for his life. "You let me live, and you'll have one more mouth to praise you." Why doesn't he trust in the resurrection?

One matter is clear. The psalmist is again brutally honest with himself and, more importantly, with God. He wants to live, and he is not going to hide behind pious, but empty, phrases.

Further, we must remember that God has revealed more and more truth to his people as time has progressed. Theologians refer to this as progressive revelation. For example, while the truth concerning the triune God is implicitly found in the Old Testament, it isn't clearly revealed until the New Testament. Similarly, there is not a great deal of clear teaching in the Old Testament about the resurrection of the dead. The clear teaching concerning heaven awaits the New Testament. The Old Testament knows of continued existence after death but in a shadowy place known as Sheol. The psalmist was uncertain whether he could praise God from Sheol.

In any case, God heard the psalmist's prayer and answered it. As a result grief becomes joy (v. 11). The psalmist expresses his eternal thanks to God (v. 12).

We have already hinted at an appropriate use of this psalm and other thanksgiving psalms among the people of God since Jesus' coming: to create in us a heart of thanks toward God. We have, after all, much to be thankful for to God. I would be so bold as to say that we have more to be thankful to God for than the ancient Israelites had.

We have, after all, a clear vision of the salvation which God bought for us on the cross. We have been saved from that ultimate evil—death—and can read in the Gospels how God accomplished our deliverance by offering his Son on the cross. Jesus Christ is the one who "has destroyed death and has brought life and immortality to light through the gospel" (2 Tim 1:10). How can we neglect to render our thanks to our Lord Jesus Christ?

Epilog

After examining how to read the Psalms, we have been able to look at only three psalms. A short melody indeed! But these psalms may be the opening bars of a great spiritual symphony contained for you in the Psalms. And, if nothing else, I hope that this book leads you to see that there are inexhaustible riches in the Psalter.

Go to the Psalms when you are happy and everything seems right with you. Sing laments to God when your life seems to crumble. When God hears your prayer, don't forget to thank him for his kindness. When you are frightened, be encouraged by the psalms of confidence. Heed the psalms of wisdom. Above all, go to the psalms to be honest with God.

This, and much, much more, is to be found in the Psalms.

Notes

Introduction: An Invitation to the Psalms
[1]These quotes are taken from H. Lockyer, "In Wonder of the Psalms," *Christianity Today* 28 (March 2, 1984):76.

Chapter 1: The Genres of the Psalms
[1]For a more technical and fuller discussion of genre, see my "Form Criticism, Recent Developments in Genre Theory, and the Evangelical," *Westminster Theological Journal* 47 (1985):46-67.

[2]H. Dubrow, *Genre*, Critical Idiom 42 (London: Methuen, 1982), p. 1.

[3]This is an allusion to the recent debate among evangelicals sparked by the publication of R. Gundry, *Matthew: A Documentary on His Literary and Theological Art* (Grand Rapids: Eerdmans, 1982).

[4]For examples, consult H. Gunkel, *The Psalms* (Philadelphia: Fortress Press, 1967); C. Westermann, *Praise and Lament in the Psalms* (Atlanta: John Knox Press, 1981); E. Gerstenberger, "Psalms," *Old Testament Form Criticism*, J. H. Mayes, ed. (Austin, Tex.: Trinity University Press, 1974), pp. 179-224; W. Brueggemann, *The Message of the Psalms* (Minneapolis: Augsburg, 1984); and P. D. Miller, Jr., *Interpreting the Psalms* (Philadelphia: Fortress Press, 1986).

[5]A point made by C. Westermann in his *Praise and Lament* as well as his *The Psalms: Structure, Content and Message* (Minneapolis: Augsburg, 1980).

[6]For a helpful study of kingship in the Psalms, consult J. H. Eaton, *Kingship and the Psalms* (Naperville, Ill.: Alec R. Allenson, 1976).

[7]Westermann, *Praise and Lament,* pp. 25-30.

Chapter 2: The Origin, Development and Use of the Psalms

[1]For a good explanation of the rest of the titles, consult D. Kidner, *Psalms 1—72* (Downers Grove, Ill.: InterVarsity Press, 1975), pp. 32-46.

[2]B. Duhm may be taken as a scholar who represents such a view.

[3]The titles begin with an infinitive construct prefaced with the preposition *beth.*

[4]B. S. Childs, "Psalm Titles and Midrashic Exegesis," *Journal of Semitic Studies* 16 (1971): 137-50 and E. Slomovic, "Toward an Understanding of the Formation of Historical Titles in the Book of the Psalms," *Zeitschrift fur die Alttestamentliche Wissenschaft* 91 (1971): 350-81.

[5]Kidner, *Psalms 1—72,* p. 46.

[6]This is a position earlier argued by E. J. Young, *Introduction to the Old Testament* (Grand Rapids: Eerdmans, 1949), p. 301.

[7]In *The Psalms in Israel's Worship* (Nashville: Abingdon, 1962).

[8]For instance, in his commentary, *The Psalms,* Old Testament Library (Philadelphia: Westminster Press, 1962), particularly pp. 35-52.

[9]H.-J. Kraus, *Worship in Israel: A Cultic History of the Old Testament,* trans. G. Buswell (Oxford: Basil Blackwell, 1966) and most recently in his *Theology of the Psalms,* trans. K. Crim (Minneapolis: Augsburg, 1986).

Chapter 3: The Psalms: The Heart of the Old Testament

[1]Quoted by J. Anderson, "Introductory Notice," in *Joshua. Psalms 1—35* by John Calvin, Calvin's Commentaries 4 (reprint ed., Grand Rapids: Baker Books, 1981), p. vi.

[2]Ibid., pp. v-vi.

[3]C. S. Lewis, *Reflections on the Psalms* (Glasgow: Collins, 1961), p. 10.

[4]For more information on covenant, consult the books by Dumbrell, Kline, McComiskey and Robertson listed at the end of the chapter.

[5]This is a point made well by J. Murray, *The Covenant of Grace* (London: Tyndale Press, 1954).

[6]The work of M. G. Kline has forcefully shown this connection; see his *Treaty of the Great King* (Grand Rapids, Eerdmans, 1963); *By Oath Consigned* (Grand Rapids: Eerdmans, 1968); and *The Structure of Biblical Authority* (Grand Rapids: Eerdmans, 1972).

[7]O. Palmer Robertson, *The Christ of the Covenants* (Phillipsburg, N.J.: Presbyterian and Reformed, 1980), p. 15.

Chapter 4: A Christian Reading of the Psalms

[1]R. Beckwith, *The Old Testament Canon of the New Testament Church* (London:

SPCK, 1985), pp. 105-9.

[2]Ibid., 126.

[3]D. Dunbar, "The Biblical Canon," *Hermeneutics, Authority, and Canon* (Grand Rapids: Zondervan, 1986), p. 306.

[4]A. Harman, "Paul's Use of the Psalms," (Th.D. diss., Westminster Theological Seminary, 1968), p. 2.

[5]This is similar to the interpretation argued by P. C. Craigie, *Psalms 1—50*, Word Biblical Commentary 19 (Waco, Tex.: Word Books, 1983), pp. 158-59.

[6]This chapter owes much to the brief but stimulating comments of E. Clowney in "The Singing Savior," *Moody Monthly* 79 (1978), pp. 40-43.

[7]R. Vannoy, *Covenant Renewal at Gilgal: A Study of I Samuel 11:14—12:25* (Cherry Hill, N.J.: Mack Publishing Co., 1977).

[8]Clowney, "Singing Savior," p. 42.

Chapter 5: The Psalms: Mirror of the Soul

[1]I have omitted a separate section in this chapter on the imagination. In our investigation of imagery in the Psalter (chapter eight) we will get a glimpse of the Psalms' appeal to the imagination.

[2]J. Calvin, "The Author's Preface," in his *Joshua. Psalms 1—35*, xxxvi-xxxvii.

[3]S. G. Meyer, "The Psalms and Personal Counseling," *Journal of Psychology and Theology* 2 (1974):26.

[4]J. H. Gelberman and D. Kobak, "The Psalms as Psychological and Allegorical Poems," in *Poetry Therapy*, J. J. Leedy, ed. (Philadelphia: Lippencott, 1969), p. 134.

[5]J. I. Packer, *Evangelism and the Sovereignty of God* (Downers Grove, Ill.: InterVarsity Press, 1961) and S. Ferguson, "Election," *Know Your Christian Life* (Downers Grove, Ill.: InterVarsity Press, 1981), pp. 102-15.

[6]D. A. Hubbard, *Psalms for All Seasons* (Grand Rapids: Eerdmans, 1971) and *More Psalms for All Seasons* (Grand Rapids: Eerdmans, 1975).

Chapter 6: Old Testament Poetry

[1]Stanza 1 from "Astrophel and Stella," *Sir Philip Sidney: Selected Prose and Poetry*, R. Kimbrough, ed. (New York: Holt, Rinehart and Winston, 1969), p. 163.

[2]For the literary nature of biblical prose read R. Alter, *The Art of Biblical Narrative* (New York: Basic Books, 1981); M. Sternberg, *The Poetics of Biblical Narrative* (Bloomington: Indiana University Press, 1985); and my *Literary Approaches to Biblical Interpretation* (Grand Rapids: Zondervan, 1987), chapters five and six.

[3]Different scholars use different terms to describe the poetic line. Sometimes it gets quite confusing! For instance, I use *poetic phrase* to describe a part of a "line," while some others use *colon* or *stich* for the same thing. The best I can do is to be consistent with my own terminology.

Chapter 7: Understanding Parallelism

[1]The point and the example are taken from J. Kugel, *The Idea of Biblical Poetry* (New Haven, Conn.: Yale University Press, 1981), pp. 102-3. As will become clearer, I am heavily indebted to the brilliant insights of Kugel, my former teacher.

[2]A. Baker, "Parallelism: England's Contribution to Biblical Studies," *Catholic Biblical Quarterly* 35 (1973):429-40.

[3]Quoted from his *Lecture on the Sacred Poetry of the Hebrews* (1753) by A. Berlin, *The Dynamics of Biblical Parallelism* (Bloomington: Indiana University Press, 1985).

[4]Lewis, *Reflections on the Psalms*. p. 11.

[5]As mentioned in a previous note, this chapter owes much to J. Kugel, *The Idea*, including the "A, what's more B" terminology. R. Alter, *The Art of Biblical Poetry* (New York: Basic Books, 1985) provides more readings of poetry from Kugel's perspective. The application of the theory to specific passages in this chapter is my own work and responsibility.

[6]S. A. Geller, *Parallelism in Biblical Poetry*, Harvard Semitic Monographs 20 (Missoula, Mont.: Scholars Press, 1979) suggests about one hundred categories. Kugel's "A, what's more B" is so general that it rightly demands that we closely examine the two cola of a line expecting anything! To limit the categories to three or even one hundred is too restricting.

Chapter 8: Imagery in the Psalms

[1]I am leaving to one side, for the purposes of this introductory book, the question whether pure literal language exists. See G. Lakoff and M. Johnson, *Metaphors We Live By* (Chicago: University of Chicago Press, 1980).

[2]Yamm's cohort, another sea monster, is named Lotan who in Hebrew is called Leviathan. Baal also strikes down Leviathan according to the Canaanite myths discovered at Ugarit:

> When you [Baal] killed Lotan, the Fleeing Serpent,
> > finished off the Twisting Serpent,
> > > the seven-headed monster,
> > the heavens withered and drooped
> > > like the folds of your robes. (CTA 5:1:1)

(translated from M. D. Coogan, *Stories from Ancient Canaan* [Philadelphia: Westminster Press, 1978], p. 106.)

Chapter 9: Psalm 98: Let All the Earth Praise God, Our Warrior

[1]The close connection between God as Warrior and God as King may be seen in P. D. Miller, Jr., *The Divine Warrior in Early Israel* (Cambridge: Harvard University Press, 1973).

[2]See my "The Divine Warrior: The New Testament Use of an Old Testament Motif," *Westminster Theological Journal* 44 (1982):290-307; and "Psalm 98: A

Divine Warrior Victory Song," *Journal of the Evangelical Theological Society* 27 (1984):267-74.

Chapter 10: Psalm 69: Lord, I Suffer for Your Sake

[1]A. Weiser, *The Psalms,* pp. 416-17 and C. S. Lewis, *Reflections on the Psalms,* pp. 23-33.

Chapter 11: Psalm 30: Thank You, Lord, for Healing Me!

[1]In his *The Message of the Psalms.*

[2]The insight is basically Brueggemann's, but there are some helpful modifications, which I accept, given by J. Goldingay, "The Dynamic Cycle of Praise and Prayer in the Psalms," *Journal for the Study of the Old Testament* 20 (1981):85-90.

Answers to the Exercises

Chapter 1

1. *Identify the genres of Psalms 34, 55, 85, 95, 135.*
a. Psalm 34: Individual thanksgiving
b. Psalm 55: Individual lament
c. Psalm 85: Lament of the community
d. Psalm 95: Hymn, kingship psalm
e. Psalm 135: Psalm of remembrance

2. *Examine the structure of Psalm 54. What kind of psalm is it? How can you tell from its structure?*
Psalm 54 is an individual lament. As such, it starts with a plea to God for help in verses 1 and 2. The complaint section is found in verse 3. The next verse, 4, is a statement of trust. Imprecation or curse against enemies occurs in verse 5. A promise of sacrifice and a note of praise close the psalm.

3. *Not all the psalms fit neatly into a clear category. Read Psalm 40 closely. What genres can you associate it with?*
The psalm opens the way an individual thanksgiving psalm would. It speaks of a past deliverance. Verse 4 has some wisdom connections. However, verse 11 and the verses following sound much like an individual lament.

Chapter 2

1. *Read the title of Psalm 52 and then the psalm itself. How do the two relate? Remind*

yourself of the story by reading 1 Samuel 21:1-9; 22:6-23.
David here reflects on the pride and evil deeds of the wicked "mighty man."
In reference to Doeg the title "mighty man" (v. 1) is ironic since he ruthlessly
murdered defenseless priests. His tongue was like a razor (v. 2) in that his
report to Saul led to the priests' slaughter. Doeg certainly did not fear God
and "grew strong by destroying others" (v. 7).

However, realize that the content of the psalm does not make the connection specific intentionally. If we expend our energy applying this to Doeg,
then we've missed the purpose of the psalm. We need to go beyond Doeg to
our own situation. Are we like the wicked mighty man or like the one who
prospers like an olive tree?

Chapter 7
1. *Read Psalm 2 and identify the separate poetic lines. Identify the poetic phrases within
these lines and label them as mono-, bi- or tricola.*

a. **A** The kings of the earth take their stand
    B and the rulers gather together (bicolon)

b. **A** against the LORD
    B and against his Anointed One. (bicolon)

c. **A** "Let us break their chains," they say,
    B "and throw off their fetters." (bicolon)

d. **A** The One enthroned in heaven laughs;
    B the Lord scoffs at them. (bicolon)

e. **A** Then he rebukes them in his anger
    B and terrifies them in his wrath, saying (bicolon)

f. **A** "I have installed my King on Zion, my holy hill." (monocolon)

g. I will proclaim the decree of the LORD: He said to me . . . (prose in-
    sertion)

h. **A** "You are my Son;
    B today I have become your Father. (bicolon)

i. **A** Ask of me, and I will make the nations your inheritance,
    B the ends of the earth your possession. (bicolon)

j. **A** You will rule them with an iron scepter;
    B you will dash them to pieces like pottery." (bicolon)

k. **A** Therefore, you kings, be wise;
    B be warned, you rulers of the earth. (bicolon)

l. **A** Serve the LORD with fear
    B and rejoice with trembling. (bicolon)

m. **A** Kiss the Son, lest he be angry
    B and you be destroyed in your way (bicolon)

n. **A** for his wrath can flare up in a moment. (monocolon)

o.   **A** Blessed are all who take refuge in him. (monocolon)

2. *Analyze Psalm 46. Read it slowly. Group together the poetic phrases and lines which resemble one another into bi- and tricola. Analyze the relationship between the lines.*

a.   God is our refuge and strength,
        an ever-present help in trouble. (v. 1)

In this bicolon, we observe a number of ways in which the second poetic phrase furthers the thought of the first poetic phrase in this line. For one, *A* tells us two things which God is to us, a refuge and strength. The second poetic phrase adds to this thought by adding a third attribute of God. Second, the *B* line specifies *A* by pinpointing a situation in which God is our refuge and strength. He helps us when we are in trouble, right now. Also, we see a move from a metaphorical statement about God, that he is our refuge, to a literal statement.

b.   Therefore we will not fear, though the earth give way
        and the mountains fall into the heart of the sea (v. 2)

The second poetic phrase clearly heightens the thought of the first. The first phrase *therefore we will not fear* sets the tone for both poetic phrases. The completion of poetic phrase *A* and the whole of poetic phrase *B* then state two situations which the psalmist gives as representative of disasters of almost unbelievable proportions.

The first poetic phrase is more general than the second. It states that the psalmist would not fear even if the stable earth crumbles under his feet. The second poetic phrase intensifies this picture of horror, especially from the point of view of the ancient Israelites. To them, mountains were the epitome of stability. The people of the ancient Near East thought mountains were the home of the gods. The sea, on the other hand, was the epitome of chaos. The poet is drawing a vivid picture of the world going to pieces in the second poetic phrase and thereby intensifies the thought of the first poetic phrase.

c.   though its waters roar and foam
        and the mountains quake with their surging. (v. 3)

The case could be made that the two poetic phrases of this line are related to the previous bicolon in some way. The thought of the line certainly continues the thought of the line in verse two.

d.   There is a river whose streams make glad the city of God,
        the holy place where the Most High dwells. (v. 4)

In this bicolon, the second part of the first poetic phrase is picked up and intensified in the second poetic phrase. The city of God, which is clearly Jerusalem, is paralleled in the second poetic phrase by a reference to the temple. The temple was located on Mt. Zion and it was there that God was present in a special way.

e.   God is within her,
        she will not fall,

God will help her at break of day. (v. 5)

Here we get a departure from the pattern of bicola which we have seen in the earlier part of the psalm. This is a pivot pattern where the middle poetic phrase, *she will not fail*, is read with the first and with the third poetic phrases.

The verse opens with a simple, but profound, statement—God is present in Jerusalem. As a result of his presence, Jerusalem will not falter. More specifically, she will not fail because God will help Jerusalem at the break of day.

This verse may give us the first glimpse of the primary setting for this psalm, warfare. The picture evoked in our minds is of Jerusalem besieged but secure in the knowledge of God's presence.

f.   **A** Nations are in uproar,

   B kingdoms fall. (v. 6a)

The first part of the sixth verse presents us with a short bicolon. We observe a cause-effect relationship between *A* and *B*. The chaotic relationship between nations results in the fall of some nations.

g.   **A** He lifts his voice,

   B the earth melts. (v. 6b)

Once again we encounter a short bicolon whose parts relate to one another by cause and effect. God speaks presumably in judgment and the result is the melting of the earth. The picture of the earth melting is common in the Scriptures and describes the activity of God the Divine Warrior as he carries out his judgment on particular nations.

h.   The LORD Almighty is with us,

   the God of Jacob is our fortress. (v. 7)

The theme of God's presence is repeated a number of times throughout the psalm, for instance in verse 5. Note also the exact repetition of this verse in verse 11. We observe both similarity and variation in this poetic phrase as we have in all of the others. Two different names of God are used. The first might be better translated *LORD of Armies* and is clearly appropriate to the warfare setting of the psalm. The second *God of Jacob* reminds the reader of God's long relationship with Israel and perhaps even specifically brings to mind the times when God saved Jacob from potential defeat at the hands of Laban and Esau.

i.   Come and see the works of the LORD,

   the desolations he has brought on the earth. (v. 8)

Here the specification of the second poetic phrase may be highlighted by noting the variety of ways in which the first poetic phrase could have been followed. We are invited in the first poetic phrase to come and see (to meditate on) the works of the Lord. The works of the Lord are innumerable. We might think of creation or providence or the election of Israel. The focus in the second poetic phrase is surprising—his work of warfare in the earth. While surprising, the reference to God's warring activity fits in very nicely with the primary setting of warfare which we mentioned above.

j. He makes wars cease to the ends of the earth;
    the bow he breaks;
    he shatters the spear;
    he burns the shields with fire. (v. 9, translation mine)

This interesting line begins with a general statement about God's ability to cause wars to cease throughout the earth. Then follows three specific actions which God performs in order to rid the earth of weapons. The first two are related by means of a chiasm

the bow   he breaks
he shatters   the spear

The last poetic phrase varies from this pattern by adding a prepositional phrase.

k. Be still, and know that I am God. (v. 10a)

As we move to the conclusion of the psalm, we are struck by this monocolon. It varies from all the bi-and tricola which we have thus far seen. The difference in structure and the content of the verse make a tremendous impression on the reader.

l. I will be exalted among the nations;
   I will be exalted in the earth. (v. 10b)

These two poetic phrases are closely brought together by the repetition of the verb *I will be exalted*. The preposition following the phrase, though differently translated in English, is identical in *A* and *B* in the Hebrew. The only variation is in the last word which is the object of the prepositions, *nations* and *earth*. But even in this simple variation we see a sharpening of thought. In this case the point is that God's circle of praise gets larger. The sense is, "I will be exalted among the nations; even more I will be exalted in the earth."

m. The LORD Almighty is with us;
   the God of Jacob is our fortress. (v. 11)

We conclude with an exact repetition of verse 7.

3. *Do you see ellipsis in Psalm 47?*

In the lines which follow, the underlined words are added to represent the elliptical phrases implied in the Hebrew.

a. How awesome is the LORD Most High,
   how awesome is the great King over all the earth! (v. 2)

b. He subdued nations under us,
   he subdued peoples under our feet. (v. 3)

c. He chose our inheritance for us,
   he chose the pride of Jacob, whom he loved. (v. 4)

d. God has ascended amid shouts of joy,
   the LORD *has ascended* amid the sounding of trumpets. (v. 5)

4. *Identify the type of parallelism found in the following passages according to the six traditional categories of parallelism (synonymous, antithetical, emblematic, repetitive,*

pivot, chiastic).
a. Pivot
b. Synonymous
c. Emblematic
d. Repetitive
e. Chiasm

Chapter 8
1. *Identify the similes in Psalms 52 and 83.*
Remember that a simile is a comparison made explicit by the use of *like* or *as.*
a. Psalm 52
In verse 2 the evil man's tongue is likened to a sharpened razor.

In verse 8 the psalmist likens himself to an olive tree flourishing in the house of the Lord.
b. Psalm 83
Verse 9 begins a long series of similes. First, the psalmist likens his present enemies to the enemies which the people of God faced during the period of the Judges. He mentions the Midianites, whom Gideon defeated, in the first poetic phrase of verse 9, and then Midian's leaders are mentioned by name in verse 11. The psalmist then mentions the victory which God gave Deborah against the Canaanites led by Sisera and Jabin.

Verse 10 compares Sisera and Jabin after their defeat to refuse on the ground.

In verses 13 and 14 the psalmist continues with similes intended to beseech God to act against his enemies. First he compares them to tumbleweed and chaff before the wind. Because tumbleweed and chaff lack roots, they are pushed along by the wind. Then in verse 14 he asks God to destroy his enemies as a fire would destroy a forest or a forested mountain.
2. *Identify the metaphors in Psalms 80, 95 and 123.*
Metaphors are also comparisons but, as opposed to the simile, the comparison is implicit.
a. Psalm 80
In the first verse we encounter the familiar metaphor of God the Shepherd whose people are his flock. The same verse ends with an allusion to God enthroned in the temple upon the wings of the cherubim. This is a subtle allusion to the metaphor of God as King.

The psalmist calls on God to save them (vv. 2 and 3). In such contexts God frequently revealed himself to Israel as a warrior (see discussion on page 130).

The constant sad state of the people of God is expressed by likening their tears to their daily sustenance (v. 5).

In verse 8, Israel is compared to a vine which was transported from Egypt and planted in Canaan. This vine supernaturally grows until it covers all of

Palestine. His metaphor is carried over into the complaint section of verses 12-13 where the psalmist asks God why he permits outsiders (boars and the creatures of the field) to come in and harass Israel. He then appeals to God to return and take care of his vine—Israel.

b. Psalm 129

The psalm is a complaint, and in the third verse the psalmist likens the trouble which his enemies brought against him to someone taking a plow and furrowing his back. But God has been good to him and in the fourth verse he likens his trouble to being tied up with ropes. But God has cut the cords off his hands. That is, he has released him from his distress.

Note that the comparison in verse 6 between grass and those who hate Zion is not a metaphor but a simile.

3. *Read Psalm 124. One major image in this psalm is water. In the first part of the psalm, the psalmist's troubles are likened to overwhelming waters (vv. 4-5). Meditate on this metaphor by determining in what way the overwhelming water illuminates the depths of the psalmist's suffering.*

This is a common image in the psalms and elsewhere. It is simply understood on one level, but on a deeper level you need some information about the Near Eastern background of the image to fully understand the point of the metaphor.

In the first place, we can all understand the seriousness of being swept away by a raging torrent of water. If it is strong enough, if it is deep enough, the water will kill us. Troubles sometimes hit us like a torrent of water. Sometimes we feel as if we can handle the pressures. However, at other times all of these distresses or perhaps one really traumatic event, such as the death of a close relative or a serious illness, may threaten to overwhelm us and sweep us away.

On another level this image would have spoken even more powerfully to the Israelites who first heard it. That is because the image of overwhelming water is a reference to the water ordeal and ultimately to the Near Eastern idea that the gods of creation defeated the sea monster who represented chaos (see the comments on Psalm 69 in chapter nine).

4. *Search through Psalms 30-35, and list all the images of God which you find. Consider how great, mighty and living your God is in light of these images.*

a. Psalm 30: God is a healer.

b. Psalm 31: God is a refuge or a fortress. God is a rock.

c. Psalm 32: God is a hiding place.

d. Psalm 33: God is a shield.

e. Psalm 35: God is a warrior with spear and javelin.

You may be able to find more. I listed the most obvious metaphors. Also it is significant that each metaphor is personal to the psalmist. God is *my* healer, *my* refuge, *my* fortress, *my* hiding place, *my* shield, *my* warrior. We can take comfort that God is all this to all who love him today as well.

Guide to Commentaries on the Psalms

There is a right way and a wrong way to use a commentary. Actually there are two wrong ways. The first is to ignore completely the use of commentaries. Some people put aside commentaries because they believe that, since all Christians are equal as they approach the Scriptures, scholars have no privileged insight into the biblical text. The second error is to become overly dependent on commentaries. "These people have devoted their whole lives to the study of the Bible. How can my opinion measure up to theirs?"

The first position is wrong because it forgets that God gives different gifts to different people in the church. Not all people are equally adept at understanding the Bible and teaching it to others (1 Cor 12:12-31). The second error is wrong on the other extreme. It forgets that God has given believers the Spirit by which they can discern spiritual things (1 Cor 2:14-16).

The right way to use a commentary is as a help. We should first of all study a passage without reference to any helps. Only after coming to an initial understanding of the passage should we consult commentaries.

And we should not let commentaries bully us. Many times they will be of great help, but sometimes the reader will be right and they will be wrong.

In this spirit I offer evaluations of a few available commentaries. I am not covering all the commentaries nor am I offering a full review. I just want to give you some guidance. I should also point out that only because I have not used them extensively I am skipping some works that others have found very helpful. A notable omission from my list is Spurgeon's *The Treasury of David* written in the nineteenth century. The older commentaries (Calvin and Delitzsch) still retain great value in the area of theological reflection, but the newer commentaries are to be preferred for philological and poetic analysis.

Allen, L. C. *Psalms 100—150*. Word Biblical Commentary 21. Waco, Tex.: Word, 1983.

Allen's commentary is very helpful in the area of the structure of the psalms which he covers. He also does an admirable job of discussing the meaning of the psalm within its Old Testament context. It is one of the better commentaries on the Psalms available to the evangelical.

Craigie, P. C. *Psalms 1—50*. Word Biblical Commentary 19. Waco, Tex.: Word, 1983.

This is perhaps the best scholarly commentary available to the evangelical world. It is regrettable that it only covers the first fifty psalms. This commentary is particularly strong in getting at the meaning of the Psalms in their Old Testament contexts. The author is known for his ability with ancient languages. This study is particularly weak in seeing how the psalm anticipates the coming of Jesus and in its application to everyday life.

Dahood, M. J. *Psalms*. 3 vols. Garden City, N.Y.: Doubleday, 1965-70.

Dahood's (in)famous three-volume commentary on the Psalms is part of the Anchor Bible series. In brief, this commentary is idiosyncratic and, accordingly, virtually unusable. Dahood makes numerous emendations to the sense of the Psalms by recourse to cognate languages. Unfortunately, he has no discernible methodological justification for many of his statements. This is a good commentary to avoid.

Kidner, D. *Psalms*. 2 vols. Downers Grove, Ill.: InterVarsity Press, 1973-75.

Kidner, the former warden at Tyndale House, has produced an extremely valuable commentary on the Psalms. His comments are brief, but they are clear and packed with insight. Though readable, they distill profound scholarship. This is the commentary I recommend most for laypeople who are interested in the Psalms.

Weiser, A. *The Psalms*. OT Library. Philadelphia: Westminster Press, 1962.

This commentary focuses on the theological meaning of the psalms and is often stimulating. The orientation is Barthian. Weiser tends to go overboard with his connections with a hypothetical covenant festival.